The Third Solitude

Benjamin Libman

The Third Solitude

A Memoir Against History

DUNDURN PRESS

Some names have been changed to protect the identities of those to whom they belong or belonged.

Publisher and acquiring editor: Meghan Macdonald | Editor: Russell Smith
Cover designer: Karen Alexiou
Cover image: figure: gremlin/istock.com; Montreal: ilbusca/istock.com; paper: STILLFX/istock.com

All images courtesy of the author.

A version of "The Window" originally published as "Wind, Light" by the *Rambling*.
A version of "Wish I Could Go Back" originally published by *Liberties, a Journal of Culture and Politics*.
A version of "The Third Solitude" originally published as "Name Everything for the First Time" by The Poetry Foundation (www.poetryfoundation.org).
Translation of Marie Uguay's poem "And yet oranges and apples do exist" by Ben Libman; originally published by The Poetry Foundation.

Library and Archives Canada Cataloguing in Publication

Title: The third solitude : a memoir against history / Benjamin Libman.
Names: Libman, Ben, author.
Description: Includes bibliographical references.
Identifiers: Canadiana (print) 20240500105 | Canadiana (ebook) 2024050013X | ISBN 9781459753662 (softcover) | ISBN 9781459753679 (PDF) | ISBN 9781459753686 (EPUB)
Subjects: LCSH: Libman, Ben. | LCSH: Libman, Ben—Family. | LCSH: Jews—Québec (Province)—Montréal—Biography. | LCSH: Authors, Canadian—Québec (Province)—Montréal—21st century—Biography. | LCSH: Montréal (Québec)—Biography. | LCSH: History. | LCGFT: Autobiographies. | LCGFT: Biographies.
Classification: LCC FC2947.26.L53 A3 2025 | DDC 971.4/2805092—dc23

We acknowledge the support of the Canada Council for the Arts and the Ontario Arts Council for our publishing program. We also acknowledge the financial support of the Government of Ontario, through the Ontario Book Publishing Tax Credit and Ontario Creates, and the Government of Canada.

Care has been taken to trace the ownership of copyright material used in this book. The author and the publisher welcome any information enabling them to rectify any references or credits in subsequent editions.

The publisher is not responsible for websites or their content unless they are owned by the publisher.

Printed and bound in Canada.

Dundurn Press
1382 Queen Street East
Toronto, Ontario, Canada M4L 1C9
dundurn.com, @dundurnpress

For Eva Libman and Joan Yess Kahn.

And for Israel Libman and Amnon Kahn;
may their memories be a blessing.

And did the Countenance Divine,
Shine forth upon our clouded hills?
And was Jerusalem builded here,
Among these dark Satanic Mills?

— William Blake

Contents

Prologue

What Thou Lov'st Well Shall Not Be Reft from Thee

"His sufferings were unspeakable. Here, look upon a man who was more tormented than Job!"
Who? Bontsha wondered. Who is this man?

— **I.L. Peretz, "Bontsha the Silent" (trans. Hilda Abel)**

Three voyagers are lost at sea. They have been for quite some time — for longer, in fact, than any of them can remember. So long indeed, that none of them knows how they wound up at sea, nor where they were trying to go.

Without instruments for navigation, they are forced to follow the stars. They crane their necks in every direction, looking for a sign. "There!" says the first traveller, pointing up and starboard. "Do you see that?"

The other two travellers shake their heads.

"There," repeats the first. "Look. I see Orion!"

After a moment, the second gasps. "Oh!" he says, pointing to the same spot as the first. "Well, I see the Giant!"

The third, following along, remains silent. The others look at him expectantly.

"So?" says the first.

Silence.

"Do you see the Giant?" says the second.

"Or better yet," adds the first, "Orion?"

The third says nothing. In fact, he does see something: the handle of an adze, clear as day. But for a while he says nothing. His speech is weighed down, for they have been out there for quite some time, knowing not how they got there nor where they are going. All they know is the boat, one another, and the sea. Some part of him understands that they have always been at sea, and for all he knows always will be. And so he is silent for some time, staring at the sky.

The others think he sees Orion, or else the Giant.

In fact, he sees the handle of an adze.

They look at him expectantly.

"So?" the first says.

"I don't see a thing," the third traveller says, "except the stars."

I wonder what it is like to see the stars, rather than Orion, the Giant, or the handle of an adze. That is what this book is about: dissolving common patterns — resisting pattern-making habits — for the sake, simply, of seeing. What then?

The patterns I care about are characteristic of history: the grand histories of nations, but also the trifling histories of personal memory. In *The Origin of German Tragic Drama*, Walter Benjamin wrote that "ideas are to objects as constellations are to stars." Many have seen it fit to extend the analogy: *as history is to the past.*

To connect each dot and to form from those connections images and stories is something we have always done. It is a natural human reflex, perhaps the only one possible in the face of the great sobering fact: that we are on our own, lost at sea, knowing not how we got here nor where we should point our boats. The past is our dome of stars, and despite lacking any transcendental destination we project onto those stars the signs that will give us the illusion of making sense, of following meaning, and therefore of going somewhere meaningful. But each of us should be troubled by the contingency of these images, by the fact that I see a Giant where you see the handle of an adze. The question of which of us is right gives way quickly to the disquieting truth that neither of us is.

The past tells us very little of its own accord; we are the ones who make it speak. Afraid to be alone with meaninglessness, we manufacture a voice, a chorus, to keep us company. What if, instead, we were to content ourselves with our own company, the gentle rocking of our boats, and the quiet, immaculate canopy overhead? What else might we see?

The past I am trying to see in these pages, shorn of its constellations, belongs to the world that made me and that remains a part of me. This is a world populated by Europeans and North Americans, Jews and gentiles, francophones, anglophones, and allophones; it is home to my family, friends, teachers, lovers, enemies, and acquaintances, all of whom will appear before you in some form or another. It is a world created in part by those who, like my great-grandparents, left another, older, world behind, in order to escape destruction during the last world war (or after surviving it). The first traveller in me might call it a post-Holocaust narrative; the second, a Jewish coming-of-age tale; the third, remaining mute for a while, might see a paradise lost. But, as if telling himself otherwise might change his relation to the world, he says: "I see the past."

The parable of the three travellers was told to me by a Georgian woman in a Berlin bar some years ago. Appropriately, some doubt in me remains as to its true meaning. But it reminded me of a fragment found in one of Kafka's notebooks: "The world will offer itself to you to be unmasked; it cannot do otherwise, it will writhe in front of you in ecstasies." For once, channelling the third traveller, I am skeptical of Kafka's claim. I've undertaken this book on the conjecture that, if we resisted just long enough, this writhing might stop, and the offering might dissolve. Because maybe the past isn't offering itself to us at all. Maybe the writhing is all in our heads.

◈ ◈ ◈

My first, ill-advised attempt to constellate the stars came on New Year's Eve a few years ago. I was in the Laurentians, at the house that my great-grandfather Eugene, an Austrian-Jewish refugee, had built on land he had purchased from the Quebec government for a bargain,

Anna and Eugene on the Rax Plateau, 1937.

in the middle of the last century. Having grown up in a nature-loving part of the world, and having spent much of his youth in the Austrian mountains and woods, or fishing lakeside, with his beloved wife, Anna (before all that would be taken from them), he had longed, so it is said, for the quiet and sylvan splendour of rural Canada.

My aunt was reading in the armchair she always read in; my uncle hovered at the hearth, stoking the fire. My brother Eli was typing something on his laptop at the small table in the far corner of the room, his face illuminated in a bluish glow. In the kitchen, those preparing drinks for themselves were listening to bolero. There were still five or six hours until midnight, and I had just resolved that I would write the story of our family.

I would explore in that story some home truths: what it means to be disfigured by suffering, to be flattened by ill fortune, yet to go on living as if one had merely drawn the wrong lot — as if good fortune, equally likely, lay just over the horizon. If only one kept living for it. It is the subject of the book of Job, and of the famous I.L. Peretz story in which a man named Bontsha, who remains utterly silent and without complaint as he endures the slings and arrows of fate before his death, is too meek even to ask for his due reward when he is offered it, unconditionally, in Paradise.

Nor were these themes exclusive to literature and scripture. I had inherited them from teachers and community elders, from institutions, individuals, parents, cousins, friends, ghosts, folk tales, old saws, and old jokes. From a packet of letters, administrative documents, and a few photographs belonging to people I knew from family histories but had never met. I knew them the way I know Odysseus and Oedipus, characters who recur across tales and tellers, always with a difference, yet always bearing a set of persistent, inalienable qualities, characters whose actions live somewhere between the imperfect and conditional tenses — what they *would do* then or would do now.

Henry and Jetka, pictured above at a wedding, were two such characters. Their stories — that is, their suffering, their lot, their inalienable qualities — had become lore long before my birth. As I fantasized about my family story, I hadn't understood this as a problem. But it was, and it remains so. Not a problem in ethical terms, but in epistemological ones. Legend and history both interfere with the past. Most of all, they interfere with each other: like oil and water, they cannot be assimilated. They can, at best, be suspended one within the other, a slurry of stubborn isolates.

I have been told many things about Henry by many different members of my family. They don't always line up. I could see this as strange for a matter of fact: a thing either was or wasn't; a man either did this or that. But when you compare accounts on any human subject you find that the differences have less to do with verifiable data than with the comparably more fluid matter of relationships. Henry was Eugene's brother. He was my grandmother Eva's uncle. He was great-uncle to my father, his siblings, and many of his first cousins. What is at stake for each of these people when they tell you about Henry is their relationship to him; the truth that matters is the truth that obtained between them. This is the truth that gets recorded in memory; dates, facts, and figures are as if incidental, sometimes brought into alignment thereby, not the other way around.

What I will tell you here is also a certain kind of truth. When as a young man, Eugene moved to Vienna, Henry moved to Lemberg, the capital of Galicia, now Lviv. There he married Zina, and the pair had a daughter, Theresa, known to all of us as Tecia. They also had a son, Richard. Then, as always, the war. I will tell you later how Eugene managed to get out of Austria while the getting was good. But we're talking about Henry now. Henry, Zina, Tecia, and Richard were sucked into the vortex. Richard, just a child, was sent to hide among Christians; he was found, at some point, and murdered by an SS officer. ("It wasn't something talked about much," my father tells me, in the passive voice, which is the only one appropriate to the subject matter. "We kids only knew the story because Henry had a boat that had his name on it, 'Rys.'") Henry, Zina, and Tecia went the way of most of the continent's Jews: labour and concentration camps. They were separated early on and, somehow, all of them survived. Henry had managed at some point to escape the camp where he had been relegated to work and die and went to live with the partisans in the forest. It is said that he forged documents, mostly passports and other identification papers. At the end of the war, he looked for his family. Today we are ignorant of the utter havoc that was finding loved ones, the formlessness of that particular panic. *Tohu va-vohu,* as the narrator of the Torah says. Dead or alive, each person would have to be traced (hence the name of the agency to which Henry appealed, the International Tracing

Service), their movements mapped to ghettos, camps, train cars, mass graves, and death marches across mainland Europe. This took time, but it was done. It took even more time if the people being sought had died or survived behind what was now the Iron Curtain. By the time Henry found out that the two people in the world most important to him were alive in Eastern Europe, he was already in Canada, where he had been reunited with his brother, Eugene. He was already trying to live life again, having suffered life's iniquities. He who, like all the Jews he had known, had been more wronged than Job. He was already married again, to a woman named Stacha.

At the time the above photograph was taken, he was still married to Stacha, and despite knowing that Zina and Tecia were alive and well, he had yet to be properly reunited with them. It was his niece Ada's wedding. And rather than join the procession with his wife, he did the *menschlich* thing and walked arm and arm with Jetka, Anna's sister (and so Eugene's sister-in-law). Jetka was, in the above photograph, a widow. Like Anna, she had come to Canada

Ignatz and Jetka, in Canada by the lake.

just before the war, and after it was over had agreed to marry a man whom she did not know, a man named Ignatz, who had lost everyone he had known and loved, and whom Eugene and Anna wanted desperately to help emigrate to Canada. Jetka had married him for a visa; they fell in love nevertheless, or so certain letters between them attest. He was dead within a decade. Someone may someday write their story.

When Henry was reunited with his wife Zina and his daughter Tecia in Montreal, in 1967, he was in the eyes of Jewish law polygamous. His first wife and daughter moved into the spare apartment of the duplex where he and his second wife, Stacha, lived. Together, having suffered what needed to be suffered, they seemed to have decided to suffer no longer. Rather than quarrel, they coexisted. They lived one on top of the other, dined and travelled together. Surely there's a Jewish joke out there about a man who the Lord has decided should have not one but *two* wives. But I don't know it.

The book you hold in your hands is not the story I rather sophomorically resolved to write a few years ago. I did write it, a fictionalization of Henry's postwar life, and it sits somewhere in the cloud. But in exorcising my subject I discovered that something vital remained within me. What was past, that is, what had really been and what had really happened, remained unattended to. I thought that I ought subsequently to work on a true account of who these people were and how they lived. But this too, of course, was a fiction. All of history is a fiction, an Orion or a Giant. If we can agree on the events, we have no way of relating them one to another without some invention of our own. The sun has risen every morning and has set every evening, as Hume pointed out. But we cannot deduce from abstract law that it will do the same tomorrow. We build inference upon inference, and suddenly we have told the story of the past. But something besides remains, for the past will never be exhausted by our exertions upon it. It refuses the way an object refuses.

This book is a meditation on the past that persists: the Henrys and Jetkas who remain fundamentally unknown, impenetrable obscurities, arm-in-arm, treading the soft carpet, smiling forever before the lens; the experiences, regrets, hopes, disappointments, vacillations of feeling, flutters of happiness, dreams, and fears that we can never touch, only represent. All of it so much air escaping to the wind. If I have not stopped fictionalizing, I have stopped trying to exhaust. Something vital remains, cold and unspeaking as a stone. Do not strike the stone, so the cautionary tale goes, though water may pour forth thereby. Speak to it — softly, gently, inaudibly. Speak to it without words.

◈ ◈ ◈

I realized some time ago that the black hole is the only appropriate metaphor for the ways in which we approach ineffable experiences. The experience itself admits no light; it is unrepresentable. But ringed around it is a shimmering event horizon of language, of the words those experiences have not yet swallowed up and made unavailable to us. The greater the weight that experience has in our culture — death, loss, epiphany — the greater the horizon that attends it. How many paeans have been sung to Love? And how many of these has Love not outstripped?

There is a black hole at the centre of this undertaking — a book about the forces of place, time, and character that formed the world and the generation into which I was born. I did not know what it was until I finished writing, but it will be plain to all who traverse the pages that follow. Its pull will be felt. The words that ring around this gravitational collapse will be familiar: Zionism, Israel, the Jewish homeland, war, catastrophe, resurrection. The passage of time. In addition to being real words denoting concrete things, they are also the symptom of the yearning, disordered soul within many a heart. The experience they attempt to index, when they are not weaponized in support of war or occupation, runs right through a people's history, swelling here to an explosive point, subsiding there to an inaudible lull.

The generations spanned in these chapters have tracked the movement of this feeling, which is another way of saying that what Israel meant then is not what it means now. The Jerusalem we have invoked at the end of our Passover seders since the Middle Ages, the Jerusalem of "next year in Jerusalem" and of the Diasporic condition that has been at the centre of Jewish life since the eighth century BCE, when we were taken into Assyrian captivity, is not the Jerusalem of the Zionist Congresses, nor that of 1948 or 2025. Two thousand years of exilic culture — marked, to be sure, by occasional homecoming for some — could not easily assimilate the prize against whose lack it had defined itself.

"They produced the miracle of Israel," is how my great-grandmother, Anna, put it in a letter to her sister-in-law. Words whose meaning is foreign to me; I am incapable of looking at Israel today and seeing a miracle; I am incapable of looking at Israel today and feeling anything but shame. But I have to attend to her phrase, to the word "miracle": a vague word, belonging to the vocabulary of the event horizon, a reach exceeding what can be grasped, a leap into the vapour of the metaphysical. She, who could never have imagined such a reality, had no language adequate to her awe. (Just as I would be mute in her place.) All the more reason for her to go on trying to capture it, in letter after letter. "I don't think it is possible today to fully understand the meaning of the state of Israel to that generation," my father said to me recently. "It is possible to understand in theory, but not the emotion. I often looked at my grandparents and thought, how can they even get through a single day? Where did they put all that sadness? Because I never saw it. Except once, with my grandfather, at Yad Vashem." He was referring to a time when, as a thirteen-year-old, he went with Eugene on a trip to Israel. They visited the National Holocaust Monument, which was not even twenty years old at that time, and which I would visit myself a few decades later under very different circumstances. "I think we stayed for twenty minutes, then he made some excuse why we had to leave." My father didn't know whether Eugene wanted to leave because it was too difficult for him, or because he thought the material not suitable for a boy. But in hearing this story I was reminded that, to Eugene as to Anna, the very idea of building a memorial to Holocaust victims in a Jewish state was a triumph over history — over temporality as such. It was a way of saying that, finally, they were safe from the ravages of time. The long exile was over.

◈ ◈ ◈

A month ago, on a trip home for Passover, I was telling an old friend about this book. I explained that I was revisiting some of the things we were taught as children, lifting the corners of the ideological system in which we were raised. I assumed he would get it. Like me, he had moved away from home, had sought things he couldn't find there. He frowned. "What are you doing?" he said with great disappointment. He meant: Why would you betray your own community like that? I didn't have an answer for him.

Whether and to what degree this book is a betrayal is not something I can determine. I can only say that I was raised by people who warned me never to take anything in this world on faith, and always to question what you were told. I have to believe that they did not exclude themselves from being subject to scrutiny. At Passover we speak of the son who does not know how to ask. His sin is not that he is ignorant but that he does not care to know. And yet he must not be abandoned — we must take his hand as we take the hands of others and lead him along. Daily, innocent people are dying as a direct result of the miracle for which Anna would spend half her life finding the right words. Is it not ours to wonder why, in the face of so much agony visited upon an uprooted and subjugated people, so many remain silent, and so many seek its furtherance? How many simply do not care to know? Give us your hands.

An entire world of collective effort, generations of it, go into crafting the attitude of a single mind. I have tried to gather that world and its generations here. This is a world, and these are the generations to which most everyone in this book belongs, including myself. If I have betrayed them now, I have not betrayed who they might yet become. I would call a statement like that credulous if it weren't one of the oldest tenets of the faith: each of us is responsible for repairing the world. It is not an act of hate, but an act of love. And, to borrow the words of a wise and wicked son, what thou lovest well remains.

The rest is dross.

Paris, 2024

Chapter 1

The Window

When we have gone the stone will stop singing

— W.S. Merwin

I

If a photograph is like a time capsule, a tribute that one pays in the present to the future, then what you see before you is a capsule within a capsule. Standing, as if at the balcony of a first-floor apartment, a mother, her husband, and their two daughters preside over a small gathering. The woman's eyes are cast downward, the white of her blouse drawing a neat line to its scintillating twin, the hat of a young girl, the object of her gaze. Her husband looks ahead, at the lens, at the viewer of this photograph months or years or decades hence. Four figures, below, look on with him. Something happening to the side has caught most of the other gazes, except two: one, the other woman in white, who also stares at the young girl; and two, toward the right-hand side, a woman who appears as if she is looking beyond the gathering,

All together.

perhaps trying to envision a navigable passage between the group and the train.

Yes, this is a train. This is September 16, 1938, Vienna central station. And this is a family. The man to the far right is the brother of the woman with the downcast eyes. The man to the far left is the brother of her husband, whose hand grips the top of the window frame and whose armpit forms an alcove over his daughter's head, the kind of space-making gesture that comes naturally to a parent. They are on a journey — north, as the sign below indicates — a journey that will take them out of Austria, annexed six months earlier by the Nazis, and toward Hamburg, where they will board a boat to take them far away. Their family, those on the ground, have decided to stay. This is the last photograph they'll take all together. The three young girls in the photo — two sisters in the window and their cousin down below — look distractedly to the side, to what is not captured. Each of them has hold of something, the one gripping the window's edge, the others holding some object or garment close to their chests.

They are separated by space and also by time. The girl below will be lost to those above for many war-stricken years. The old gentleman beside her, the father of the dark, bowtied husband in the window, will, not long after striking this stalwart pose, at the outbreak of war, die. (Across many generations in his family a rumour will persist that his sons poisoned him — secretly, sweetly — so as to spare him from being captured.) In fact, everyone down below, save four of them, would be dead by 1945. And those four who would make it would never be the same. A thick bar, set in rigid relief against the bolted tank-like metallic siding of the train, runs horizontally along this familial division. It says, "You must be this tall to ride." Those above are called back by the black depth behind them, into which they will soon recede. Perhaps the window will go up, and this small unit of four will sit down and set their gazes in parallel with the train's motion. Like the *Voyager* spacecraft, they will soon shoot down the long track and into the future, for the future.

But this capsule is different; time goes on within it. Perhaps the man takes out four sandwiches, prepared before the long ride. The woman might pull out a pen, some paper, and an envelope, setting down a message in German that she will send to her brother, on the far right, and his wife; a message that might fore-echo, like a premonition, what she would write to them at a later date, not long after arriving in Canada. What question, asked of her dozens, if not hundreds of times, might she so urgently need to attend to?

"Why did one leave? That is an impossible question," she would write. "Note," she continues, "not a question which is impossible to answer, but an impossible question. We will not leave. Or, leave what? Time is not locked to place, or not always. It has been cut loose. Sometimes, in order to keep up with time, in order to stay with it, you must run after it. If from under your feet you watch the world evacuate from itself, can you rightly say you haven't moved at all, haven't left?"

The rule of genealogical growth is the rule of the exponent. Here, it is just the opposite. Those in the window triangulate the greater number below into a pair: two young girls, the bottleneck through which the promise of these ghosts must one day pass if it is not to evaporate for good. One of those girls, the one who grips the window and directs her gaze somewhere beyond the frame, somewhere she is about to leave for a very long time, the one on the left — her name is Eva. She is my grandmother.

◈ ◈ ◈

In his essay "Berlin Childhood Around 1900," Walter Benjamin devotes a portion of his attention to the loggias that lined the inside of Berlin's many courtyards. He writes, "Later, from the perspective of the railroad embankment, I rediscovered the courtyards. When, on sultry summer afternoons, I gazed down on them from my compartment, the summer appeared to have parted from the landscape and locked itself in those courtyards." Before his eyes, Benjamin sees a commonplace structure, a specific geometry whose configuration allows it to capture, maintain, and breathe life into that quivering, ephemeral, airy substance that has since past — summer. This, it seems to me, is a vision of history. The historian finds herself not only in the process of selection, but also of arrangement. She does not recreate the past, but rather arrays its delicate fragments, in the echo of an echo of Stonehenge, in such a way as to trap the right light, or to make the wind that winds through it whistle. And it is this wind, and this light, this ephemeral illumination of a constellation of meaning, this substance that is not proper to the historian's arrangement, but that could not be called forth without it, that constitutes the coming-into-being of history.

A few years ago, I travelled to Vienna to meet a distant relative of Eva's. Toward the end of my stay, I received from her a large stack of photographs, letters, and miscellaneous documents belonging to the woman in the window — Anna Sternschuss, my great-grandmother — and her brother Max, on the far right. They had for decades been in the possession of Max's widow, Risa, who stands just beside him.

Among these papers was the letter, quoted above, that Anna wrote to Max and his wife at some point after the moment captured by the photograph below. Since my visit, I have slowly approached the task of going through these documents, translating them, and

doing the constructive or reconstructive work that, it seemed to me, one's family history demands. Vainly, I have tried not to write them into history, but rather to play with the many possible luminous arrangements of my family genealogy. In going through Anna's documents and calling forth a life — a life that is not my own and yet is the absolute prerequisite to my own — there is no hope of reconstructing some historical truth or reality as it pertains to a family. One must look instead, as Benjamin did, for that brief bit of summer that, from time to time and in just the right spot, grazes the landscape of the present.

II

What is it that we can hope to capture, to make still, when putting a history together in this way? What does it mean to foreground patience and attention, to be like the fisherman who wants to see the fish on his line, to notice the way the light plays and cascades along its scales with every undulation of its struggle for breath, before returning it (always returning it) to the murky, impenetrable current, the only mark of its brief excursion being a small hole in its lip that will soon heal?

If we are not careful, the photograph of the Sternschuss family at the train station risks being implanted with significance. When the historian is rather like the real estate speculator, every artifact is evaluated as a plot of land, as a site with potential, upon which she can erect a definite structure of meaning. We have an idea, an existing narrative, of what 1938 was in Austria. We feel the tug of temptation, the itching desire to overlay our categories: the poor souls below are among "six million," the lone four above, in the perfect quantitative reduction they represent, are counted among the "survivors." The latter or those like them will be invited to synagogues and the lobbies of tree-planting funds to say prayers for the

The dock.

former. They or those like them will stand before the congregation as the rabbi intones, more or less, "Here is Eva Libman, née Sternschuss, and she is a survivor, though not a survivor like Ernst over there, whom we might say is in a rather different category. He was in Auschwitz."

If we are not careful, we will say that the image of the train signifies the branching moment of survival, that if you look closely at its negative, you will see the swastika and all its entailments. This is the misstep we take when we stultify our historical arrangements; this is the error of trapping the past in the cage of its future. The challenge is to spring a leak in the dam of historical narrative, to empty it of its festering contents and to retrieve, from the bottom of its newly hollow distention, the moment as such. And yet this moment, frozen like a fly in amber by the photograph, cannot be penetrated nor accessed as it was. It is stubborn, and at best we cannot be sure of its capacity for speech. How to stop speaking to our artifacts, stop breaking the shell for the sake of the nut, and instead let them speak to and through us: that is the challenge.

"Dock kiss, 1925." This is what's written on the back of the photograph above. Anna sits between the legs of a man named Eugene, the same man pictured in the window of the train. His eyes are fixed on hers, perhaps on the bridge of her nose. She is so close to him that he goes cross-eyed trying to fix his gaze. Their cheekbones meet, and their mouths hover together within the space of an inch, the way that mouths that have kissed before, the one knowing the cracks and contours of the other, are wont to do. Anna looks on at something beyond the frame, or maybe at the crest of Eugene's cheek. He embraces her with all four limbs, with the entirety of his body, like an ape, holding her shoulder with his left hand, saddling her hip with his left leg. Their heads are dry, and yet the dock is covered with the watermark that footprints make on old wood. Perhaps they've gone in already and are being dried off by the sun, which imperfectly streaks the surface of the water behind them. Or maybe they're waiting to warm up before taking the plunge, and Eugene will soon remove his dock shoes and step into the cool water.

They grab hold of their own shins, just beneath the knee, as if to keep this bodily arrangement — put together imperfectly but held at the joints by a desire that reveals itself in the slight tension of the fingers that grip and take hold — from coming apart, perhaps in time, perhaps only right there, on the dock that might cradle back and forth with the minor current of the lake beneath it.

Neither one of them seems keen on moving, and yet the posture of the embrace is taught and marked by the implicit knowledge that relaxation would be its undoing. Anna's legs spill forward in a cross, out of the triangle of her lover's lap. Physically, she must get up before he can, and for the moment her body gives no hints as to when that will be. The image tells us of the delicate tenderness of love, a bond that trembles into existence and always keeps its eye on its own extinction, lying just beyond the frame. She is summer, flowing idly like liquid through his courtyard.

Placed beside the image of the train, the two flicker like the embers of an exhausted fire being reignited by a lungful of air. In both, we see Eugene — Genek, as he was affectionately called — performing the architecture of love, ensconcing Anna (on the dock) and his daughter Ada (on the train) in an arrangement of limbs that is neither inhibitive nor unzealous. The hand that grips the window glows as the chiral image of that which grips the shin, a mark of the trusswork that bears the load of time, that allows the line of family to touch down periodically in a stabilized containment.

Train, close-up.

And yet, as we gently nudge these two moments together, it is the figure of Anna that smoulders and radiates most intensely. Ever the centripetal locus, the object of the viewer's gaze, her eyes betray the fact that her mind wanders elsewhere. The lens and the occasion of the photograph seem not to register with her. She looks down, or beyond; her eyes track the world as it evacuates itself from beneath her feet, not only in times of war and trauma, but also in times of love, in times of summer; at all times. The world falls away like wet sand being drawn out into the rip current, the only mark of its receding force being the heels that have sunk deeper into the terrain upon which they meant only to tread.

In September 1964, Anna, sitting in her study in Montreal, will write to her sister-in-law: "The season is fading, the drudgery of work goes on. Summers here are brief and intense, and they call out their rapid descent into autumn with a single, cold day, usually in mid-August, the herald of what's to come! It reminds me of those years in Vienna and with Genek. Everything seemed so good and bright. And they were. But the good makes one uneasy, and makes [one] feel rather like a decadent Roman jolted out of his daydream in the bathhouse by the call of a barbarian war horn … The presentiment of the bad creeps in. You sense that there will be arguments and tears right when things couldn't be more splendid. Autumn is already in the summer! Though by no means does one sense how bad it could all become."

III

"'Having been there' — both as a newcomer and a psychologist dedicated to the cause of uprooted people, I feel particularly obliged to write down my memories of the years mentioned above."

This is the first sentence of a letter titled "A Backward Glance at the 1940ties," which Anna sent to the rabbi of her Montreal synagogue, the Temple Emanu-El, sometime in the 1960s. Spurred, it seems, by the rabbi's particularly edifying sermon given a few weeks earlier on the issue of the cultural integration of new immigrants, the aim of the letter is to expound on this topic from her first-hand perspective.

"During Eva and Ada's first year of school here," Anna writes, "they came home one day and began to perform a strange ritual, almost like a dance, which required the contortion of their arms into various sharp angles and the incantation of the phrases, 'I'm a little teapot, I'm a little teapot. Here is my handle, and here is where the water comes out.'

"I had spent much time during our voyage to Canada worrying about the girls and their ability to integrate. But such is the sweetness of children that they assimilated more quickly than I did! — so quick, in fact, that I was completely bewildered by their little dance and didn't know what to think!"

The letter goes on to enumerate Anna's long journey toward what she calls cultural integration. In our family, we know this journey well: she earns her Ph.D. in psychology; each of her daughters marries; she learns French and befriends Viktor Frankl, whose work she translates for the Université de Montréal; she and Genek buy a house in Notre-Dame-de-Grâce, a middle-class neighbourhood of the city; she more fully picks up English, her sixth or seventh language, and wields it confidently in many of her letters. "Although by no means immune to many of the troubles encountered by newcomers in Canada," she adds, "I and my family were lucky to have certain educational and professional advantages, which made it a lot easier to cope with the difficulties inherent in the situation of 'a stranger among strangers.'"

◈ ◈ ◈

The file for the photograph below reads, "Grandpa and Granny, '7?" For whom is that question mark given? To whom does this artifact pass, like a clue haunted by an imprecision, an approximation, a dot to be connected, the blank in a vast archive? Did Anna, who would die in 1982, write this to herself, hoping that in her final moments she might recall, as if by epiphany, how and where this piece of her puzzle falls into place? Or was it for Eugene, who would live another seven years, wanting more than anything in his loneliness to spend time with his grandchildren and to see the birth of his great-grandson, my brother Max?

As it turns out, the question mark was a computer error. It was the product of no one's mind; the moment of the photograph — a

The gaze.

fiftieth wedding anniversary party — is not a matter of uncertainty. And yet I cannot shake the question mark. It is as if, by way of a cosmological glitch, the typographical certainty by which we would normally stamp time with a date was obstructed. Maybe we retain the mark, not only here but everywhere we see an image. Maybe we refuse the imperative to find its answer and insist instead on its fundamental ambiguity, on its being and remaining a question. Perhaps the point is not to moor this or any moment in time, to scan for its place in the index of a life, but rather to let it float free, to let it emerge osmotically through the pores of the past.

How does this image shimmer, then?

The two are in the twilight of their years. Genek sits back, his lips curled over his teeth in a chuckle, his silver hair still full and combed past his ears in a controlled mane that tapers briefly like a comet, his paunch well-satisfied with years of plenty. His hands disappear from the frame, relaxed, no longer gripping. He stares off to the side, to something or likely someone beyond the frame soliciting his merriment.

Anna sits more upright; not tense, but attentive. Her hands, too, are invisible. They are covered by the odd arrangement of apples and wine on the table before them, a rectilinear still life that summons the memento mori inherent to the photograph, to any photograph. A large Magen David, painted or plated with gold, hangs from her neck, its weight accentuated by the acute V that it coaxes from the thin chain on which it hangs. The scene, someone's garden, is lush and verdant, dappled with a warm light that glistens smoothly on Genek's forehead and kindles the faded red of Anna's hair. They've been married fifty years, but the image resists our breathless catalogue of what they've "been through." We are called only to look, to be drawn toward the image's well of gravity, steep and sudden like that of a dying star: Anna.

Her gaze is turned on us, but it is not finally so. Released from the narrative of history, which seeks the language of development and of culmination, she does not find us only now but has always already found us. It is not her gaze that has learned to look, over time and through trauma, at the stationary lens, but rather our own, which has learned to seek hers where it falls. Her eye is everywhere on time as it recedes into the past, beyond the dock, but also into the future, the young girl in the glowing hat. To meet her gaze, we need only complete the inaccessible task of leaving the lens and placing ourselves there, in the rip current of time. And this image, in beautiful colour that accelerates from a streak of blue into a blur of green, affirms this point emphatically, hauntingly. The chance meeting of the lens with Anna's almond-brown eyes marks our perfect, circumstantial untimeliness, our view through the pipe of time and the many holes a stare can burn through it.

◈ ◈ ◈

The day Anna died, May 9, 1982, was warm and bright. Sitting in her study, whose windows overlooked a calm, tree-lined street in Notre-Dame-de-Grâce, she pulled from the typewriter the final page of her latest book, a sociological study of the cultural integration of Slavic Jews in Canada, and left it standing in the paper rail, the other two hundred or so sheets squared in a neat stack on the table. She rose, walked to the room's threshold, announced to her husband down the hall that she was going out, and stepped outside for a stroll through the neighbourhood. The streets, no doubt, glittered in the sun. Columns of light poured over the parks, the playgrounds, the spiral staircases that snake up the facades of many Montreal apartments. The squirrels must have raced each other up each tree as she passed. I try to picture her, to place her. What was she thinking then? On what did she set her pensive gaze?

When she returned home, she set her things aside, shuffled into her study, and sank back into her chair. She closed her eyes and would never open them again.

Chapter 2

Days and Hours

I do not think that they will sing to me.

— T.S. Eliot

I

I came into possession of some of Anna's photographs and letters on a trip to Austria ten years ago, under strange circumstances. My journey there was not unmotivated: I needed to meet someone whom, until recently, I hadn't known existed. And so I boarded a train from Milan to Vienna on a warm Sunday morning in August without knowing what the journey would bring.

I had been travelling through Germany and northern Italy with my then-girlfriend for over two weeks. Freshman year had just ended, and despite her pleas, I had resolved to transfer to a different university. There were good reasons for doing so. But the truth, as I see it now, and as I did not quite know it then, was that I needed to get away, to unbind myself from the obligations that tethered me to others. Campus was a stultifying place, and I felt as if the opportunity to go to a big city somewhere, to disappear among strangers, had been lost to me. As I recall we fought much of the trip. But there were good, silent moments, long meditations on cool trains overlooking the pacific waters of the Rhine, the craggy, tan cliffs of the calanques dropping straight into the Mediterranean, seabirds cutting across the shore along the Côte d'Azur. We ate well, slept deeply, washed the dirt from our skin in blue waters.

But nervousness was taking hold of me. My leg shook constantly. She asked me how often we'd see each other, now that we'd be several states apart, and I could answer only that we'd figure it out. For the first time I was regularly experiencing the symptoms of what I would later learn to be panic attacks: a sudden elevation of the heart rate, a tightening of the chest, hyperventilation. Years later, on a highway in California, I would finally succumb to one of these attacks in full. I would pull onto the shoulder of the 101, near exit 414, and would stumble out of my car into the heat and roar of the open freeway. I would call 911 and insist that I was having a stroke, so severely would the hyperventilation have produced muscle spasms in my face, chest, and limbs.

"We'll figure it out," I said to her several times. All my life I have been figuring things out; every situation is an object for the future perfect: it *will have been* figured out. The only question was how.

◈ ◈ ◈

In Civitavecchia, watching four boys fling themselves over the steps to the beach on skateboards, I received an email from Marta. I had been waiting to hear from her for over a month. Or, I'd been hoping to hear from her; I wasn't sure the email address I had been given was really hers. But now there was no doubt: she was inviting me to see her in Vienna. I could stay at her home. I raised a glass of Campari to my lips and held it there, peering out toward the water from behind my sunglasses. The ice cubes had melted; the drink was warm, oversweet, unpleasant.

Marta was known to my father's family, though I had never met her. No one, in fact, had met her, though my father had met her sister, and my grandmother had met her mother. Until I received that email, written half in English and half in German, punctuated by a *Grüß Gott!*, she had been less a person to me than an idea, a sign. On the floor of the apartment in Paris where I am now living, and where I am writing this sentence, there is a dark mark no larger than a coin set into the wood. It looks exactly like a natural scar from any old knot. But if you knew it intimately, as I do, you'd know that it was formed by the glowing end of a fragment of *palo santo* wood I had been burning as incense, some weeks ago. Marta — the sign, more so than the person — was just such a mark in the woodwork of our family. By all accounts she was simply a distant relation. But to us, to *me*, she was something else entirely: a link to the past.

Marta was the grandniece of Max and Risa Seidner-Weiser, my grandmother Eva's aunt and uncle. Risa, who survived the war, was Anna's dearest friend from the time she married Max (Anna's brother), until the end of Anna's life. The pair exchanged hundreds of letters and thousands of confidences. Risa's niece, Ilse, was also known to us, though as a person and not merely a sign. She was Eva's cousin, and they had met before. To Risa, who had never had children, Ilse was the closest thing to a daughter.

A few weeks before I left for Europe, my father told me the story of a young Austrian woman who, sometime in the 1970s, came to visit my grandparents in Montreal. This was Marta's sister, visiting to meet the Canadian kin she had heard whispered about now and then. Her visit was the only point of contact my father would have with a part of our family that might otherwise have been familiar to him, had Eva never been chased out of Austria, and had he grown up with German on his tongue. It was also around this time, shortly after the sister's trip, that Ilse and Eva grew more distant. This wasn't very hard to accomplish; they barely spoke as it was. But, as I understood it, there was little desire on the Austrian side for a restoration of family relations. The mystery of *that side* devolved into one of our old family stories, rarely if ever recounted, an appendage whose true function had been lost to time.

Eugene (*second from back*), Anna (*third from front*), and friends. Austria, before the war.

Eva did what she could over the years to retain knowledge of the Austrians' whereabouts — where they received mail, how they could be reached by telephone, relevant email addresses, not much else. When my father told me the story of Marta's sister, during a dinner at my grandmother's house, I asked her whether she knew where she was or how to reach her. She smiled politely and muttered an answer in the negative. But a couple of hours later, she handed me a sheet with an email address.

II

On the journey from Milan to Vienna the windows were pelted by heavy rains. After a tight transfer at Verona Porta Nuova, I found myself a window seat and tried to rest my eyes. There were about eight hours left in the journey. I had confirmed with Marta a few days earlier that I would be arriving at 9:00 p.m., but she had yet to write back saying whether and where she would meet me. I pulled out my phone, opened the Mail app, and tugged down on the inbox. The wheel spun but wouldn't refresh. I was out of credit on my prepaid SIM, and the train's Wi-Fi was not working. My leg shook; I peered around. At length, I slept.

A sudden jerk. Screeching. Several people were thrown against the seats in front of them. After a few prolonged moments the train car came to a halt and the grumbling people inside, me included, pressed their noses against the windows to see what was going on. There were green fields interrupted by patches of stunted forest on either side, black specks of distant cows along the far dale. We waited. After a few minutes, a voice crackled through the PA, saying something in Italian, then in German. I couldn't understand what was announced, but I inferred from the groaning and the abrupt hand gestures that we were stalled indefinitely.

The old man beside me, seeing that I was confused, or perhaps having picked up on my mother tongue from the novel I had been reading, told me, Car accident. Blocked. He smiled. I nodded and smiled back. After a while, a train attendant came through our car, not intending to stop, and endured the many delays to his particular mission occasioned by the handful of frustrated and inquisitive passengers wanting more information. Eavesdropping on the hushed conversation between him and the four French travellers behind me, I learned that the car blocking the train, which we might have hit, was a small hatchback. I checked my phone for the time: 7:00 p.m., so, two hours until I had said I would arrive. Maybe an hour until sunset.

I stared out the window and watched the sun approach the distant hills, and then spread across them like molten iron. As everywhere in Europe, the land beyond the train was parsed into pastures, acres of furrowed soil, fields of crops. A year before, a French friend had visited me in the United States, and as the two of us drove across a particularly sad and empty stretch of American country, his face was glued to the window in awe: he had never seen so much *land*, so much unowned and unworked territory. *La campagne* meant something completely different to him. I was coming to appreciate the European way, the sense that no matter how far one had strayed from civilization, one was never lost. One could always, while escaping some threat, say, run to the nearest farmstead, find shelter in the barn of a stolid, morally upstanding farmer. How gently the dirt roads cut into the patchwork of the Austrian land! How inviting the evening light sending shadows pooling into grassy dimples.

I tried to read the novel in my lap. A land surveyor alights in a foreign town and takes shelter at a local inn. He has been summoned there by the town's authorities, who operate out of the nearby castle, but he has not been told how to get in touch with them now that he has arrived. He attempts, through various intermediaries, to reach the castle, to determine what goes on there, but is at every turn thwarted. Or, not quite thwarted: deviated, turned onto a path just slightly divergent from the one he was intent on taking. Despite not knowing what, exactly, occurs in the castle, the townspeople speak of it with great reverence, praising it for its faultless bureaucracy. But the land surveyor, enervated, knows this to be untrue: he has been summoned precisely because of a flaw in some paperwork that has its origin in the castle. He has been called — by whom, or what, he does not know — to address a fault in a faultless place, which he cannot, at any rate, manage to access.

With the train's engine and electricity shut off, the carriage began to grow hot. I put down my book and scratched at my torso. Somewhere at the front of the car, or in the back of the next car, a baby started crying—screaming, in fact, so hard that it was gasping for air. The passengers shuffled uneasily in their seats. I felt my pulse rise, slowly, swelling like a wave, and gripped at the underside of my legs. When a panic attack looms, the difference between it overtaking your body and it withdrawing is entirely a function of how you acknowledge it. You cannot speak its name in your mind, cannot look at it head on. Like the Gorgon, it will paralyze the one who stares into the serpent-ringed eyes. But it cannot be ignored, either — for it is seizing you, trying to claim you, and it will not stop until you greet it: customarily, tactfully, strategically. You must gaze upon it as if through the peripheral vision of your mind, allowing it to skirt the borders of your nervous system, peer into your heart, sniff around like a beast, and then be on its way. You breathe, you lock your eyes onto something else, you wait for it to depart. You breathe, you look, you wait. You breathe, you look …

In the distance, a white speck moved like a fly across the meadowland. It began to burn orange, reflecting the sun's weaker rays out into the countryside, gliding steadily closer to us. The dot developed into an object, a white van, kicking up dust as it sped into view. The red cross on its side door materialized and the word ƎƆИAJUᗺMA revealed itself above the windshield. The van disappeared from view somewhere in front of the train. We waited.

About thirty minutes later, with the light almost completely gone, another dot emerged along the country road, this one much larger. The tow truck lumbered into view before long, its huge yellow arm bouncing as the cab traversed the uneven ground. Clapping started up among the passengers, spreading down the adjacent cars. One or two people even hollered when the tow re-emerged bearing behind it a Citroën C15, driverless, the pair of vehicles now linked and retreating back toward the shallow dale.

At last, the ambulance inched back into view, climbing the divot by the tracks and levelling itself on even ground. The driver parked, opened his door, and jogged back to open the rear doors. A minute later, a pair of paramedics pushed a yellow, elevated stretcher up the hill. On it was a body completely covered by a white sheet. The men collapsed the stretcher and lifted it into the van. A moment later, the vehicle started up again and sped off the way it came, its silent lights flashing blue, a beacon diminishing into the thick gloaming.

As the grey and black boxes of industrial buildings gathered in volume on either side of us, I realized that we'd be approaching Vienna Central Station in a matter of fifteen or twenty minutes. Against my feelings of social anxiety, I woke one of the sleeping French travellers behind me and asked her if I could borrow her phone to make a call. She was quite beautiful and tall, and when she awoke to my backlit face, startled, she instinctively covered herself with her cardigan. *Tiens*, she said, handing me her phone. Reading through the old emails on my phone with one hand, I tried the number listed under Marta's automatic signature with the other. It rang and rang, but no one picked up. I opened the internet and tried searching her name, *Marta X. Wien*, but her surname was far too common. *Puis-j'envoyer un mail?* I asked the traveller. She took a second to think and said no, reaching her open palm toward me. I returned to my seat and gripped my knees.

The city slid vaguely into view, a low mist hanging over the lampposts and buildings, the streets half visible in the haze. We lurched into the station under bright sodium lights and waited for the PA to announce our arrival. Slowly, like sleepy children, the passengers got up and slid their arms into their light summer jackets, reaching for their bags and briefcases in the open compartments that ran along the carriage ceiling. The group of French travellers retrieved several large, purple suitcases from the baggage containers at the back of the car. I rubbed my eyes, passed a hand through my hair, and stood up, patting my jean pockets for my phone and wallet, patting my jacket pockets for earphones and gum. I slung my rucksack over my shoulder and trudged down the carriage with the other passengers, feeling the blood return to my legs. The doors hissed open. I stepped out.

I connected to the station Wi-Fi and sent Marta an email, then waited on the platform until it was empty. At length, the train pushed back again without any passengers, rolling slowly into the darkened reaches of the railyard where empty trains go. Across the track, pasted on the far wall of the station, was a large poster, an image of a figure suspended in mid-air, tied with a bungee cord to a tall crane. There was nothing else on the image: no text, no logo, no QR code. Just the falling figure. My leg began to shake.

It was now midnight. No response from Marta. I took out my wallet and counted my money, about thirty-five euros. Surely, that could get me a night at a hostel. I opened Google Maps and began sifting through the hostels reachable by foot from the station. I

called three of them via WhatsApp; all of them had a tired, irritable teenager working the front desk, and none of them had any room. I tried calling the A&O Hotel, just down the street, but no one picked up. So I walked there. The man at the front desk was sleeping, his feet stacked on top of the counter. Could I get a room? Yes, I could. How much? Thirty-seven euros. I told him I had thirty-four and change, but he refused to take it. I told him I could get the remaining few euros the following day, if he'd just let me sleep the night. I handed him my Casio watch with the cracked screen as collateral. He lifted it to the light and frowned. For me? he asked. No, I said. Only until I bring you the other three euros. He laughed. No, he said. Sorry.

I walked back to the station, as the mist lifted and turned to rain. A homeless man was now sleeping on the bench where I had earlier been sitting, so I walked to the farthest end of the platform, looking for my own bench on which to lie out. But it became clear that the first bench was the only one in the station that didn't have armrests splitting the seat in four, a widespread tactic for preventing

so-called illicit sleeping. It was getting chilly, so I pulled a sweater from my rucksack and slipped it on.

The ground, spotted with the black chewing gum from another decade, would have to do. I lay my bag crosswise and rested my head upon it. Using my jacket as a blanket, I tried lying on my back, but the overhead lamp was too strong, so I turned onto my side. On the wall across the track, I could make out the same poster as before, only this one had been pasted upside down. The figure appeared to be hovering, floating like an astronaut in weightless space.

I closed my eyes and imagined her movements, dreamed of being unbound by gravity or any other weight, tethered only to the mothership somewhere out of frame. I thought of the man in the ambulance, his body bouncing beneath the white sheet as the van trundled its way across the pastureland. Where would they go, I wondered. The ambulance must return to whatever hospital it came from. But the body — what use is an old body in a place like that? And why turn on the flashing lights if the man is dead? To send a signal, a message, or whatever. His body rolls and rumbles in the back cabin and the paramedics' faces are illuminated on either side of him, each telling his beloved that he will be home soon, or later, each scrolling through the dreamlike fabric of the internet. Meanwhile, as the train departs and the hills pull back along the conveyor belt of relative motion, I catch a glimpse of him, the real *him*, his phantom rising like a winter's breath from the place along the tracks where, right at the strangest instant, he coincided with his fate. He rises and rises, his diaphanous form stretching gently on the passing breeze, dispersing itself into gossamer air and cloud. At the last instant, giant and warped, he opens his mouth, forming a gigantic O through which a train in the sky might pass, as if he wants to tell me something. And just as he is about to speak, his O becomes a 0, and then a ||, and we lose sight of one another in the sleepy alleyways of the night.

I was awoken by a persistent nudging on my right shoulder. Bleary-eyed, I turned my head and saw a silhouetted figure, its head haloed by the lamp above. I skittered backward, nearly rolling off the platform and onto the tracks. The figure was startled by the sound I had made and moved farther away from me. Slowly, as my eyes adjusted, I made out the face of a woman framed by red hair, pulled back into a bun. She had one hand to her chest, controlling her breathing. The other was dangling by her side, gripping a shining pair of keys to a Mercedes-Benz like a weapon.

She spoke my name. I could not tell if she was asserting it or asking it. I extricated myself from my jacket and stood up, carefully. I still could not quite see her, backlit as she was. Who is that? I said, though I knew. She said my name again, this time with the clear inflection of a question. I stepped forward to reach out for her, to turn her from the light, to see this Marta with fresh eyes, but

I stumbled and found instead that I was once more caught in the void, the pitch, the formless space of my dreams, the unbounded walls echoing with the sounds of my name.

III

It was early in the morning when we pulled into Marta's driveway. The house before us was so tall that I had to lean forward to find the roofline through the windshield of her car. She turned off the engine. "Home," she said.

The vestibule gave way to a series of large rooms with off-white walls, dark wooden furniture, curved floor lamps with bulbous shades, Berber carpets. Before bidding me enter, Marta stopped for a moment by the table in the hallway to watch sped-up CCTV footage of her front door. She had been expecting a package, she said, and it was odd for it not to have been there when we arrived. "The Poles, sometimes, you know …" She deposited her keys in the perfect circle of a brass dish and proceeded to give me the full tour.

Marta had two children, both boys, one of whom was only a bit younger than me and the other a few years younger than that. The eldest was away at a boarding school in Scotland; the youngest dreamed of fishing in Alaska and used his bedroom to develop photographs (though Marta told me where he was and why he would not be home during my stay, I instantly forgot). There are people who want you so badly to know what their children have accomplished, or what they spent their most recent vacation doing, or what they saw in their dreams last night, and who have no idea how tedious all of this information is to anyone outside their own heads, or anyone as self-absorbed as I was at eighteen. Marta kindly showed me to the guest room, where the bed had been made up by someone with professional experience and the window gave a grisaille view onto the rooftops of Vienna, its earliest risers just beginning to stir and prepare to do it all over again.

I got up around noon, startled by the sound of grass trimmers nearby. I had been dreaming about a story that my father had once told me. In fact, in this dream I *was* my father, in a story being told *by* my father to me when I was thirteen or fourteen years old. When he had finished college he embarked on a year abroad with his closest friend, David. Together they cycled across Europe, sleeping in tents or in farmers' fields and eating what they could find or afford with the few francs or lira or schillings they could rustle up. (Years later, before starting my freshman year, I would be inspired to replicate this trip in a way, touring France and parts of Switzerland and Germany by bicycle with a school friend of mine.) My father worked at a ski repair shop in Verbier and, during the summer months, as a lighting technician in a Viennese theatre.

In the story in question, the one that my dream seemed to repeat three or four times over, I — that is, my father — found myself cycling alone somewhere in Landes, pushing my way up a hill against pelting rains with fifteen kilograms or more in my saddlebags. This was one of those stretches when David had split ways to chase a skirt or pursue some more wholesome touristic vision. Alone, then, I crested the hill, stopped by a ditch, pulled a creased and weathered Michelin map out from my windbreaker and strained to calculate the distance between myself and the nearest town. It was about forty kilometres, which in finer conditions wouldn't pose an issue. But I was soaked through both layers and through my socks, and I was beginning to shiver and turn blue. Pedaling slowly, the rain smeared against my glasses, I scanned for farmhouses until I spotted one on my lefthand side a couple of kilometres away. A long gravel drive led to the front door of the house and, not wanting to lean my bicycle on the newly painted white balustrades of the porch, I laid it on its side across the path. I knocked, then rang, and eventually a man of about sixty or sixty-five opened the door and looked me up and down. I explained my predicament and asked if I could pay him to spend the night. He scowled, disappeared inside, and re-emerged having decided to let me stay in the barn, sleeping on the hay bales, on the condition that I left at sunrise. I thanked him and followed him up the natural footpath to the barn, where I stashed my bike against an empty cow stall and shook the man's hand. He closed the doors, telling me to bar them against the impending winds. I sat hunched upon the bale that was to be my bed, my eyelids heavy and my pulse thumping, and devoured the soggy half-baguette that had been poking out of my saddlebag. I lay down, shoes and bike gloves still on, my wet clothes sticking to the hills and valleys of my rib cage, and fell asleep.

I awoke to the sound of banging. It was so dark I could not make out my hands, but by the shards of moonlight that defined the gaps in the wood I could see the barn doors heaving back and forth against the crossbar. The wood creaked and seemed ready to splinter. Could the wind do that? The movement stopped; I listened for the wind but heard only crickets: this was no storm. Then, the sound of shuffling feet, and again the doors began to heave in and out, a set of great, ligneous lungs. I was petrified, unable even to sit up on the bale. After a minute more of effort the crossbar split in half and the doors gasped open. I saw the silhouette of a man, standing at the threshold as if in awe at the achievement of his strength, breathing hard and steaming a little into the night air. His posture changed — he had spotted me. But oddly, he didn't seem surprised to find a man in a cow barn. He approached now, and I could hear him muttering some nonsense to himself, and within seconds he had his hands on me, on my shirt, tugging at the fabric and seeming at first to want to lift me to a seated position, then to want to remove the shirt entirely. We struggled in the strangest silence, speaking only to grunt, and it dawned on me that I would die or be raped, or both. And I thought my life had not yet amounted to enough to end. (I still think this.) Then we heard someone yell from somewhere outside. Despite this, my assailant went on trying to subdue me. The yell rose again, from near the threshold this time, and a moment later the old farmer appeared in the doorway with a shotgun raised above his head. He hollered once more, and this time I could make out that he was saying a name, the man's name, I reckoned, for my attacker finally withdrew and spat out a sharp reply. Rather than shoot the man, as I half expected, or lunge at him with the butt of the gun, the farmer simply ordered him to leave, again by name, and I watched in disbelief as the man who had just been trying to undo my existence stomped off like a scolded child, down the driveway and into the night. "Sorry," said the farmer, gruffly (was he angry at me?), before shutting the doors and leaving me, my father, in the pitch black once more.

When I descended to the kitchen, I found Marta seated at the dining table, reading something on her iPad. Before her was a spread of deli meats, cheeses, bread rolls, and mustards, all untouched and covered in cellophane. I apologized for having slept so long and accepted her offer to make coffee. Within minutes of her uncovering the platter I had scarfed down about a third of it. We chatted a little about my journey and the quality of my sleep in the guest room. She was, I was realizing, a deeply kind person. She wanted to take care of me and ensure my comfort. Sometimes this disposition is absolutely clear in people; they radiate it. Her hair was red, or perhaps it was dyed that way, and her eyes light blue. She told me more about her son, Karl, who loved Alaska, or rather the idea of it, and proceeded to ask me about Canada: Were there really so many lakes? Was the wilderness really so large? Did people really hunt and fish and camp so far from civilization that they were beyond rescue should something happen to them? I nodded with my mouth full of bread and cheese. She asked me about my family, about my grandmother and my father, and expressed how much she would like to meet them. I told her that they were excited about my being out there, in Vienna, visiting with her. (I doubted then whether my grandmother, Eva, really shared such excitement.)

The front door opened, and Marta seemed to withdraw slightly into herself. A man entered the room and, without clocking me for several seconds, began speaking to Marta (or to himself) in German while he searched the cupboards for a coffee mug. "Ah," he said, finally seeing me. "Hallo." I stood and introduced myself. "Right," he said, in English now, shaking my hand, "a relative of Marta's?" Something like that, I replied. "Hans-Ulrich," he said. He kissed Marta on the cheek without really looking at her and sat down across from me. He placed the empty white mug he had grabbed on the table, at which sign Marta rose to fetch the pot of coffee for him. I wondered for the first time in a long time what day of the week it was.

Hans-Ulrich told me that he worked in investment banking and had to live between Vienna and Munich, spending two or three days in one or the other each week. Marta, he added, gesturing to our surroundings as if in explanation, was a business administration consultant for Austrian and Bavarian corporations. He mentioned Mahler's grave, and how I could find it. He asked me to remind him where I was from, and asked no further questions after that, having exhausted his curiosity. He grabbed a newspaper from the counter behind him and began reading. Marta poured the coffee and began to relay what we might get up to that day, depending on my desires. I was surprised to hear that she had taken off the beginning of her work week to spend time with me. I told her that I'd like, above all, to see the city a bit and to try some local food. Then to do whatever else she had in mind. Hans-Ulrich raised his head suddenly and asked Marta, in German, something about a package. She shook her head. Looking at me, as if through the fourth wall, he said, "The Poles, you know … "

IV

Two poles planted on the roadside suspended a political banner asking Austrians to vote for the right-wing Freedom Party in the European Parliament elections that had been held about a month prior. Marta, holding the wheel of her Mercedes with a slack hand, gestured with the other something to the effect of, *never mind them.* The Freedom Party had picked up two seats relative to the previous election, but European Union politics were "mostly fanfare, anyway." We didn't have far to drive: Marta and Hans-Ulrich lived in the 18th District. We drove along the Danube, along which low walls ran with more old election posters. One couldn't actually see the river from the road, which struck me as a signal failure of urban planning. She pulled into a parking spot a few minutes' walk from the Figlmüller, where we were to eat.

I ordered the schnitzel exactly as it had been made and served for the past hundred odd years. While I squeezed lemon juice over everything and struggled to determine how best to cut into the parts of the schnitzel that flopped over the edge of my plate, Marta ran me through the history of the area, which consisted mostly of comments about how *this bank* had been there since the heyday of Habsburg influence in Europe, or how *that building* had once housed a famous diamond retailer. I asked her what we would be doing all day, and by way of her sinuous response I gathered that we would be eating food for several hours, making pilgrimage to the city's most venerated haunts like stations of the cross. Fine by me.

By the late afternoon I was struggling through a piece of heavy chocolate cake, known as Sachertorte (after the man, Franz Sacher, who invented it for the pleasure of Prince Metternich) in a café situated in the gardens of Schönbrunn Palace. Many of Europe's great public parks and gardens were once hunting grounds for royals. The original footprint of Berlin's Tiergarten was enclosed in 1527 for the benefit of the elector of Brandenburg; forty years later, Maximilian II appropriated the floodplains that would come to form the grounds of Schönbrunn in Vienna for the same purpose. He had perhaps been inspired by — or envious of — his cousin Philip II, king of Spain, with whom Maximilian had an uneasy and frankly rather tense relationship, Philip holding, in Max's eyes, several corrupting qualities that did not befit a Habsburg king, namely introversion and a provincial attachment to his native Spain. Max, by contrast, styled himself a worldly extrovert who claimed to put his Germanophilia in service to the empire writ large, thereby universalizing what might otherwise be deemed parochial, righting administrative and cultural wrongs wherever he set his gaze. Philip was nevertheless the first of the two cousins to expropriate a vast area of land outside his own capital, Madrid, for the purposes of hunting game. Casa de Campo is much vaster than Schönbrunn, as anyone who has visited the two would immediately know, and is better compared to the Lainzer Tiergarten on the outskirts of Vienna, which boasts nearly 2,500 hectares of land once devoted to hunting (and now devoted to wildlife preservation), compared to Casa de Campo's 1,700 hectares, and which had been enclosed by Philip's uncle (Maximillian's father) Ferdinand I, Holy Roman emperor, in 1561, less than one year before Philip circumscribed his own hunting area.

As was the custom in those days, the lands chosen for enclosure had no necessary relation to the actual, indigenous presence of animals thereupon. The Habsburg emperors and kings as well as the electors of Brandenburg all chose territories close to palaces and estates where they spent significant portions of their time, whether at court or on summer holiday, and where one might not be likely to find the kind of animals one liked to see from the other end of a bow or rifle, and so had to order that game be brought onto these lands for the purposes of their own (and their courts') amusement. Naturally, to keep the animals roaming territories unnatural to them, Europe's kings, electors, and emperors had to ask their groundskeepers and gamekeepers to fence in the grounds, lest the wild boar, fallow deer, elk, mouflons, pheasants, and quail make their meandering way back whence they were brought. This custom of faunal displacement probably emerged as common practice only over time, as ennobled counts, barons, and lords sought to emulate (most often in miniature) the manners of their kings, and as kings and queens themselves sought to replicate what their ancestors had managed to achieve with the resources and animals at their disposal — going back centuries.

Hunting for sport is, in fact, as old as or possibly older than Europe itself. The Franks, developing a custom that would later only bolster their pretension of perpetuating the true spirit of Rome, were the first to recover the Roman law claiming that to own property was to own the right to hunt on that property. The sport became so refined under the Merovingian and then Carolingian dynasties that one particularly holy Merovingian, Hubert of Liège, was canonized in 743 CE, sixteen years after his death, as the patron saint of hunters, hunting dogs, archers and bowmen, and the inhabitants of the forest. To be an inhabitant of the forest has long been an important fantasy for Europeans, especially as the commons were gradually and variably enclosed across the continent and in Britain, and as members of the Old World began to learn about the New one and the lifestyles of the Indigenous Peoples. Few saw this more clearly than the Grimm brothers, who understood the forest to be a cypher encoding the roiling unconscious of Germanic culture. The word "forest" itself, while signifying to us the general expanse of trees that covers a terrain of just about any size, anywhere on Earth, is said to derive from a Latin term for the "royal woods," or else from the medieval Latin *forestis*, denoting "forest preserve" or "game preserve." In other words, the very notion of the forest in Europe was, for hundreds of years before the Enlightenment-era explosion of public parks, identified with the aristocratic practice of hunting game for sport, a semantic hangover we are still suffering from and that one feels in a diffuse way when one stumbles upon any of those vast, manicured parks, often at the outskirts of one's city, and experiences the vertigo of the sudden dilation of space where just a few moments prior, and in fact throughout one's daily life, space was a rarer commodity than precious stone. As I write this sentence, I am thinking of the Bois de Boulogne, which is forty-five minutes away by metro or two hours by foot. The last time I was there, to see an exhibition of Joan Mitchell paintings hung awkwardly beside some late Monets, was the first time I thought to google the park's history. I learned that the Bois had been designated as a hunting ground by Phillipe-Auguste of France, also given the regnal name Philip II. He sought, more than three hundred years before the Habsburg Philip seized Casa de Campo, to revive in that section of French woodland the spirit-enriching pastime so enjoyed by his ancestor Dagobert I, last of the Merovingian kings and the first of the Frankish kings to be buried at the Basilica of Saint-Denis, where he wanted his remains to rest alongside those of Denis himself, patron saint of the city of Paris and of France, and where all but five of the kings of France, from Clovis I to Louis-Philippe by way of the headless Louis XVI, are buried. (The plurality of French kings have been named Louis, in homage to Clovis, which is an earlier version of the same name.) Unlike the Bois de Boulogne, the Großer Tiergarten, the Lainzer Tiergarten, and the Casa de

Campo park — or indeed London's Hyde Park, which Henry VIII acquired for hunting in 1536 from Westminster Abbey, which had owned the property since the Middle Ages — Schönbrunn makes no present-day pretense of being public, for the people, by nature. The palace and its grounds are, much like the Luxembourg palace and its gardens, devoted to the idea that aristocratic grandeur once predominated there, on the very spot where one now finds oneself wiping crumbs of Sachertorte off one's white T-shirt, while one's companion empties the dregs of a nine-euro cappuccino down her throat. These kinds of places are worse than ruins, being the sort of remainders that refuse to become remnants, insisting on their vitality the way hucksters insist on the qualities of their snake oil.

When we left the palace grounds, we crossed the Wien and turned onto the Linke Wienzeile, heading toward Marta's car. I was stunned when she said, rather casually, that my grandmother's childhood home was somewhere on this avenue. "I don't know the number," she said, "but it's somewhere between the Kettenbrückengasse and Karlsplatz U-Bahn stops. I think." I looked around. The buildings standing along the stretch of the Linke Wienzeile we were traversing were modern. I couldn't imagine that young girl in the train window, my grandmother, emerging from any of these doors.

A few blocks down, however, we passed in front of a building with a stone facade in the nineteenth-century style. A plaque by the front door explained that the structure had been damaged (*beschädigt*) during "the 1939–1945 war," and was later restored (*wiederhergestellt*) in the late 1950s. Could this have been her home? Well, it *could*. It offered the rough reassurance of plausibility. In some of the photographs we keep in our family, my grandmother and her parents pose in front of similar stone facades. With not much effort one could even say they pose in front of *this* stone facade. Unlike personal memory, the memory of one's family, of a story preceding oneself, does not demand of the rememberer

exactitude. I sometimes cannot sleep until I recall the exact song that was playing at the exact restaurant where I ate dinner exactly three months before. But when it comes to the narrated past, to history, in other words, my mind has few qualms about converting the plausible into the actual. What did it *really* matter if things were actually one way or another? Every story of the past, even the most fastidious, is already an arrangement of types. The *thing that happened* is superseded by *the kind of thing that would happen*. The little girl who actually lived at one address or another becomes the kind of little girl who would have lived at this sort of address.

The funny thing is that the true address of Eva's childhood home is no great mystery. She knows it; my father knows it. It is an apartment in one of two possible buildings — the only ambiguity lies in not knowing which one. At the time, walking beside Marta not believing I would ever be able to eat again, I did not know about the two addresses, but I knew that I could with a text message or a quick email exchange. Not knowing, though, preserved for me a certain crucial quality to my Viennese adventure, namely that it allowed me to turn the past into an object, to feel it like a mist lightly rolling down the streets and boulevards as I strolled through. (This is often called romanticization, which nevertheless does not feel appropriate to the story I was interested in unearthing.) This is a problem I have not yet managed to solve: how to admit that whatever occurred in the past happened the same way that things in the present happen. That they had no more intrinsic significance than do the events I live and suffer today. They were no less random, no less prone to bathos. As I write this sentence, my grandmother is alive. She speaks of the past, her past, in ways my heart resists. I would prefer the sin of overlaying my categories upon everything she would recount as a mere event (whatever that can be said to mean). How much more appealing to imagine that any one of these old buildings might have registered the faint echo of her youthful footfall, rather than to know that these and those definitely did not, and that this did.

In the evening I dined with Marta and Hans-Ulrich in the nearby hills at a vineyard specializing in Grüner Veltliner. We sat at an old picnic table and marvelled at the steaming heaps of sauerkraut, smoked sausage, and pig trotter that were placed before us. Marta wore silver rings and earrings, and let her red hair down, and placed the key to her Mercedes on the table in front of her. She asked more about Canada, this time about the Jews there. How many were there? What was the community like? I either didn't know or couldn't answer in a way that didn't universalize what was probably specific to the particular community I came from. The sun began to set, flooding the vines, and I had one of those rare and deceiving moments of overbrimming emotion at the thought that life was grand and utterly infused with beauty and purpose. There were probably tears in my eyes as Hans-Ulrich chatted about traffic in the city or the differences between Bavaria and western Austria. I felt almost as if I were their son, or else the version of myself who might have been born in Vienna had Hitler never risen to power, with parents perhaps much like these.

V

Three days later, I returned to Vienna after visiting Salzburg on my own. It was an impromptu trip designed to bring me closer, somehow, to the land that should by rights have been my own. Vienna was too cosmopolitan to be "Austrian" in the sense I had been trying to conjure for myself. I had wanted to put one foot forward and find myself suddenly in a Handke or Jelinek play. Maybe, by visiting Salzburg and placing a hand upon the yellow facade of Mozart's birthplace, in homage to the master, I could transform myself into a Bernhardian monomaniac. No such luck. Salzburg said nothing to me, gave me nothing other than the feeling that I should like to penetrate farther into the mountainous regions of the west. I overpaid for just about everything, returning to Marta's nearly broke.

The next morning began solemnly, in silence. It was a fateful day from the start. It was to be the day that gave this trip its reason for being, relegating all other days and their activities to the realm of the incidental. I found that I had finally tired of ham, cheese, and rolls for breakfast, and so ate little. I accepted too much coffee and found myself shaking all over, my knee bouncing up and down in the passenger seat of the Mercedes. The engine idled while Marta scoured the bushes in front of her home for the package she still had not received. "I'll have to write a complaint to the post office," she said while backing out of the driveway. "Or the police." The cars and

the large houses of the Ruhrhofergasse inched by without making an impression on me. I was so anxious about the day to come that I felt numb, like a patient etherized. I wondered faintly how many of these homes had once belonged to Jews. Not many, surely — but some. It was a thought I had had many times before, not only in Vienna but in Germany and Prague and other parts of Europe. And for whatever reason I tended only to have them when looking at big houses or stately apartment buildings. All the pre-war metropolitan Jews of my imagination were rich, most of all those from Vienna. They were established members of their community and their city; 2.1 million people lived in Vienna in 1910 — 125,000 of them self-identified as members of the "Mosaic confession" (a term particular to the era that captured both religious Jews and secular Jews who, though needing to indicate that they followed the Laws of Moses and not the Word of Christ, placed greater importance on their Austrian identity than their ethno-religious background). They were patriots, related not only to the 300,000 Jews who fought for the Austrian imperial army in the First World War, but to the 25,000 of that number who were officers. They were distinguished, well-to-do. They were bourgeois, perhaps because Eva's family had been bourgeois: overeducated engineers, sociologists, doctors, and psychologists, related distantly to Buber and Freud, occupying a place on the fringe of that circle that once defined Vienna as a cultural and intellectual powerhouse. They were rich but not wealthy; they probably didn't understand money very well. Both Eugene and Anna had been born in small towns whose significance was so marginal that they had spent the nineteenth and early twentieth centuries being handed off between empires and inchoate nation states like low-denomination chips that sweetened the geopolitical pot. They didn't "come from" anywhere, in effect. And so, like many members of the bourgeoisie anxious to prove — more to themselves than to others — that they belonged to their class in a way more rooted than mere fortune would grant, they affected the manners, customs, tastes, and traditions of that milieu as best they could.

And very well, I'd bet. They wore tailored clothes and handmade hats, bought subscriptions to the opera and the philharmonic, smoked pipes, filled their bookshelves with the classics and endeavoured to read Thomas Mann and other of the more respectable modernists, collected second- and third-rate works by first-rate artists, went to a chalet in the mountains on holiday, the riviera in the summer, and made connections at the local gentlemen's and athletics clubs. This Jewry was a universe apart from that which has long occupied the North American imagination: the Jewry of

Anna and Eugene on their wedding day.

shtetls, Yiddishisms, farming and poverty, roadside vendors and illiterates, New World tenement dwellers; the Jews who glided by Lady Liberty on a steamship, wool cap in hand, nose full of salt-water mist, eyes wide with expectation. (Here I must admit to running roughshod over some important nuance: about 80 percent of Vienna's pre-war Jewry were first-generation immigrants to that city, many of them poor and representing the orthodox milieu of Galicia and thus not easy to assimilate into the more secular Jewry found among the bourgeoisie; these two communities, the Reform and the Orthodox, had developed a history of mutual compromise so as to get along, going back to the 1860s, with the former agreeing to abandon the use of church organs in services, and the latter agreeing to say their "obsolete" prayers silently in synagogue.) All our Jewish jokes — the best ones, anyway — come from *this* Jewry, the peasants and the villagers, the ones who haggled over kopecks and goats. (There would be no Eugenes and no Annas in *Fiddler on the Roof*, except off-stage.) They, too, were dispossessed and killed en masse. In fact, to me, if such a thing is possible, they often had a grimmer fate: nudged at gunpoint to the steep edge of a yet-to-be-filled mass grave in the middle of a forest, in the middle of winter, naked. (I have been to one of these gravesites, where the earth is frozen mid-roil into tortuous tumps.) These Jews were a world apart from those others, who might have lived in one or two of the homes on the Ruhrhofergasse.

Eva's husband, Israel, came from that other world. His parents were Romanians who, as the saying goes, didn't have two pennies to rub together. His father, Sam, arrived in Canada as a teen and scraped by as a fruit vendor. When Israel was a child in Montreal, living on rue Esplanade a stone's throw from the Saint-Urbain Jews who would come to populate the novels of Mordecai Richler, his parents spoke Yiddish to one another, and sometimes to Israel and his sister. They kept kosher and maintained the severe domestic morality that one finds mainly in families desperate to rise out of poverty and into the lower middle class. Israel was forbidden from playing street hockey in the ruelles of the Plateau with his friends and instead forced to practise the violin. When, fresh out of college, he asked for Eva's hand in marriage, it was a genuine question: *Could* he? How would Eva's parents, Germanic and bourgeois, react to a match with a boy from a poor family, an Eastern European, a Yiddish speaker, a man who kept kosher? And conversely, how would *his* parents feel about a girl so secular she might hardly have seemed Jewish at all? Whatever the concerns, they quickly got past them. But the fact remains that Israel's family would never have been found on the Ruhrhofergasse.

This is made all the more curious by the fact that these two Jewish "worlds" often and in many parts of Europe stemmed from the same origin and only gained their mutual distinction in the nineteenth century. Eugene's family came from Tarnopol, known now as Ternopil. At the time of his birth, the city was part of Austria-Hungary, but in the time of his grandparents it briefly came under the possession of the Russians; and later, during the First World War, it was variously the property of the Germans, the Austrians, and the Russians. Tarnopol was a significant part of the region of Galicia, which was the birthplace of Chassidic Judaism and which, since the partition of Poland in 1772, had become famous as a centre for Jewish learning and culture in Eastern Europe. Extreme poverty following in the wake of Emperor Josef II's so-called Edict of Tolerance, which introduced a new tax for non-Christian empire dwellers — whose newfound freedom to study and learn trades within the empire came at a price — led many Galician Jews to seek prosperity elsewhere, especially in Vienna and Austria more broadly, where Jewish migration was heavily restricted by the edict. Eugene's family can be understood, then, as belonging to the tail end of this slow, snakelike movement from the fertile soils of what is now Ukraine into the industrious regions of the empire's capital. They, too, had once been "those Jews," the ones who would've seen themselves reflected in the jokes shouted at passersby crossing Montreal's rue Saint-Urbain for some grocery shopping. But upward class mobility is a powerful process of dissolution, at the end of which one can hardly remember where one got one's start, or how one's parents or ancestors once made their bread. Suddenly, as if waking from a coma with amnesia, one finds oneself the man-about-town, married to a woman who receives visitors in one's drawing room, listening to one's daughter practise her piano lessons. When, rolling swiftly toward the Donaukanal and the Innere Stadt, I imagined the city and its people dissolving past me in black and white, as it would have been captured back then in a photograph or a montage destined for future generations. I saw Eva and Ada and Anna and Eugene, exiting apartment buildings and waiting at tram stops and reading the menus outside of warmly lit restaurants, but I could not make myself see Israel or his parents, because they could not have been there, could not have watched their precious belongings and framed canvases hauled off by government thieves.

None of these reflections served to calm me. We were headed toward Ilse's, hence my anxiety. "My mother is very old," Marta kept saying, as if to apologize for something in advance. But what? I could only reply that I didn't mind old people, had even spent considerable amounts of time with them. The apartment building was rather squat, maybe six storeys high, but it sat on a hill and so imposed its stature somewhat as we approached. In my memory it was a wooden structure, but I can't be certain. Ilse's flat was on one of the upper floors. An eternity passed between Marta's knocking and the sound of sliding chains and clicking locks. I could hardly make out, at first, the diminutive form that appeared in the space between the jamb and the hesitantly opened door; despite it being the middle of the day, almost no light seemed to filter through the apartment into the vestibule. Marta exchanged a kiss with the old woman. I smiled and said hello.

As Ilse led us inside, I understood immediately why the light was so weak, and what Marta had been attempting to say when she told me that her mother was very old. There was stuff everywhere: newspapers, pamphlets, empty picture frames, hundreds of yellowed books stacked precariously on chairs and side tables, crumpled receipts, validated tram tickets, matchbooks and matchboxes, file folders spilling their documents like fish guts, opened envelopes, magazine clippings. A footpath was cut through the clutter in each room, showing how one might get from the sitting room to the kitchen, the kitchen to the balcony, the balcony to the bedroom, the bedroom to the toilet. It smelled like a library in a windowless room. As we shuffled through the vestibule and toward the glass doors of the balcony, Ilse asked me a couple of questions that I attempted to answer satisfactorily, despite my poor German. She had a kind face, though she didn't smile all that much.

From the balcony we could see a ways into town. Ilse served us tea, or coffee, and bid us wait as she disappeared into the darkened living room. I have tried so many times to accurately remember the rather banal scene that then followed. But for some reason, that moment, standing there with Marta on her mother's balcony, overlooking Vienna, remains partly occluded in my mind. The essentials I recall: Ilse returned in a shuffle, holding a stack of papers and white and beige folders — old folders, torn here and there at the corners — which she then handed to me. But why do I recall an old man watching us from behind a window? Was Ilse's husband not present, too, albeit at a distance? I never shook his hand, but was he not somewhere in the sitting room watching this exchange of documents? Or had he already died some years before? I remember only Marta translating for me what her mother said as she watched me flip through the papers now on my lap. They had belonged to Risa, Ilse's aunt. Most were letters from Anna to Risa and to her brother, Max, Risa's husband, many of which were posted in 1943, when it would have been too late for him to receive them. While attempting to escape the Nazis by fleeing to Spain via France, he was captured by French police. The official acte de disparition, a sort of death certificate issued by the French government in 1947, summarizes his fate succinctly: "Interned on 26 February 1943 at GURS; Transferred on 2 March 1943 to DRANCY; Deported on 4 March 1943 in the direction of LUBLIN-MAJDANECK (Poland)."*

---

* This kind of certificate was issued following Article 88 of the French Civil Code, which states, "At the request of the public prosecutor or the parties concerned, the death of any French national who has disappeared in France or outside France in circumstances likely to endanger his or her life may be declared by the courts if his or her body has not been found." Though he was not a French national, Max's death was declared in this manner because the French national rail service was responsible for deporting him to a concentration camp.

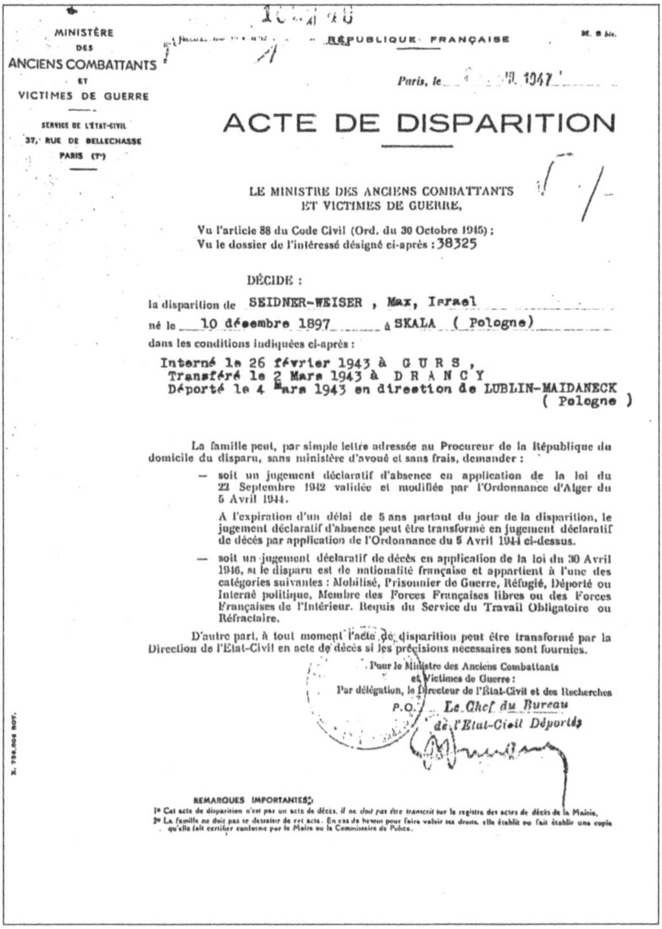

MINISTÈRE DES ANCIENS COMBATTANTS ET VICTIMES DE GUERRE

SERVICE DE L'ÉTAT-CIVIL
37, RUE DE BELLECHASSE
PARIS (7e)

RÉPUBLIQUE FRANÇAISE

M. 8 bis.

Paris, le ... 1947

ACTE DE DISPARITION

LE MINISTRE DES ANCIENS COMBATTANTS
ET VICTIMES DE GUERRE,

Vu l'article 88 du Code Civil (Ord. du 30 Octobre 1945) ;
Vu le dossier de l'intéressé désigné ci-après : 38325

DÉCIDE :

la disparition de SEIDNER-WEISER , Max, Israel
né le 10 décembre 1897 à SKALA (Pologne)
dans les conditions indiquées ci-après :

Interné le 26 février 1943 à G U R S ,
Transféré le 2 Mars 1943 à D R A N C Y
Déporté le 4 Mars 1943 en direction de LUBLIN-MAIDANECK (Pologne)

La famille peut, par simple lettre adressée au Procureur de la République du domicile du disparu, sans ministère d'avoué et sans frais, demander :

— soit un jugement déclaratif d'absence en application de la loi du 22 Septembre 1942 validée et modifiée par l'Ordonnance d'Alger du 5 Avril 1944.

A l'expiration d'un délai de 5 ans partant du jour de la disparition, le jugement déclaratif d'absence peut être transformé en jugement déclaratif de décès par application de l'Ordonnance du 5 Avril 1944 ci-dessus.

— soit un jugement déclaratif de décès en application de la loi du 30 Avril 1946, si le disparu est de nationalité française et appartient à l'une des catégories suivantes : Mobilisé, Prisonnier de Guerre, Réfugié, Déporté ou Interné politique, Membre des Forces Françaises libres ou des Forces Françaises de l'Intérieur, Requis du Service du Travail Obligatoire ou Réfractaire.

D'autre part, à tout moment l'acte de disparition peut être transformé par la Direction de l'Etat-Civil en acte de décès si les précisions nécessaires sont fournies.

Pour le Ministre des Anciens Combattants et Victimes de Guerre :
Par délégation, le Directeur de l'État-Civil et des Recherches
P.O. Le Chef du Bureau de l'Etat-Civil Déportés

REMARQUES IMPORTANTES :
1° Cet acte de disparition n'est pas un acte de décès. Il ne doit pas être transcrit sur le registre des actes de décès de la Mairie.
2° La famille ne doit pas se dessaisir de cet acte. En cas de besoin pour faire valoir ses droits, elle établit ou fait établir une copie qu'elle fait certifier conforme par le Maire ou le Commissaire de Police.

X. 738.006 ROY.

The somewhat ambiguous "in the direction of" is not a product of bureaucratic vagueness. It represents an actual uncertainty, as far as official documentation goes, as to where and when Max died. Had he arrived at Majdanek, he would have had, at best, about a 25 percent chance of leaving the camp alive; his name would also have been recorded among the arrivals in the meticulous train records kept by the Nazi camp administrators. But as far as the French

Ministry of Veterans and War Victims could tell, Max was never recorded as having arrived at the camp where, today, one can stand before a mountain of human ashes heaped inside a concrete, open-air monument to the dead. Another way to put this is that he almost certainly died while on a train operated by the same national rail service that operates trains all over France to this day. His corpse may even have been dumped overboard or left to some unwitting attendees at one of the many rural train stations between France and Poland. In any case, his remains will never be found.

The photograph below, used presumably for some sort of identity card or document, was among four or five similar headshots

included in the pile Ilse gave me. My father and uncle also have copies of this same headshot, indicating that he had ordered several prints of it, or else that they were printed multiple times on a single sheet of photographic paper, before being cut out one by one. There were also postcards, newspaper clippings, and dozens of legal and administrative pages dating back to the nineteenth century. Most bore text or lettering in German, though many others were in Polish, Russian, French, and other languages I couldn't identify. It was known in my family that Risa had been a hoarder, and it was evident that the stack I now held in my hands had been collated not by Ilse herself but by her aunt and was only left to the former for safekeeping or as part of the legacy in Risa's will. I sifted carefully, using the opportunity of being with two germanophones to identify the nature of as many of the items now in my possession as possible. One of these was a curriculum vitae for Carl Weiser, one of Max's maternal uncles, written in 1900. "I was born in Cernowitz in 1855, attended school in Leipzig between 1864-1865 … " Twenty-five years after writing this CV, Carl would go on to found the first language school in Vienna, which would make him a somewhat known quantity in Viennese respectable society, a fact about which his many family members would be proud, as evidenced in their correspondence, which I held in my hands.

Though it was clear to me from the start that these documents were now mine, or more accurately my family's, for some reason I protested that I couldn't accept such a significant gift. In fact I had known beforehand that something like this would happen: Marta had told me, the night before, that her mother wanted to give me something. This accounted for my nervousness in the car and presently accounted for my illogical unwillingness to accept the offering. It was as if I were being given a responsibility I did not want, because I did not know what to do with it. Was I supposed to have everything translated? Or maybe I was meant to scan and preserve it all for posterity? Ilse suggested that I donate some of the more interesting papers to the Jewish Museum of Vienna. "Risa already did this once," she told me, "but she always said she probably missed something." I considered that document hoarders, being squirrelly with information but lacking the assiduousness of record-keepers, always knew *that* they had without necessarily knowing *what* they had — I could well imagine Risa's erstwhile certainty that she had "probably missed" something even as she could not have pinpointed what that something was. Every family has its amateur historians and its genealogists. My father is one. Eva's nephew, Eric, is another. And by all accounts Risa was one, perhaps the first, having found herself in the peculiar position of one who felt the catastrophes of the Holocaust while being untargeted by them herself, on account of her Christian faith and Austrian ethnicity. Her husband was taken from her by her own leaders, who thought her the ideal of purity. And that man, Max, had disappeared in the worst way imaginable: vanished in a question mark, in the space between one railway station and another, in the black ink of the words "in the direction of." How could she have ended up as anything other than a hoarder, a searcher, a detective chasing a mystery long-ago solved? All she wanted was to fix this ambiguity to a definite spot, a fact. I think Risa hoarded in the hope that somehow, someday, one of those errant clippings or carbon copies was going to prove itself to be the missing piece of her life's puzzle. She wanted control. My father had told me that she chose to die by assisted suicide. She travelled to Switzerland for it. Maybe this was why: a matter of control.

◈ ◈ ◈

I left Ilse's with the certainty that she was happy. For once, something she had been holding on to had lived up to its reason for being preserved. This was a parcel whose transit had not been spatial but temporal; and, to her mind, it had now arrived at its destination. She was rid of it. And now I was burdened. Sitting in the passenger seat as Marta pulled out of the driveway and rolled us toward home, I fretted at the weight now pressing upon my lap, trying with both hands to keep its sheets and slips from being jostled out of order and onto the car floor.

That evening, I was treated to another of Ilse's gifts. She had asked Marta to give me one of her season tickets to a loge in the Wiener Staatsoper. It was my first time seeing *The Magic Flute*. Not having brought any nice clothes, I attended in jeans and a short-sleeved shirt with buttons. I was transported by exhaustion into a reverie, paying little attention to the performance unfolding before me. But the essentials made it through. I wished that such a flute could be granted to me: a guide, an aid, a talisman to bring me through the trials of my life, where I felt lost and unready to bear the weight of duty. But it was an empty thought. The next morning, having bid Marta farewell, I heard the ringing of the previous night's music finally leave my mind's ear. I could feel myself emptying out as I walked toward the central train station, bound for Paris. I was reducing all my thoughts, seeking what, if anything, remained. And there, irreducible, was the load now added to my back, the legacy of which I was now the custodian. I had only the one thought left: *What to do?*

Actually, this is not true. I had one other thought, which lingered in spite of all. It was the memory of something Ilse had said to me right before we left her apartment. It was a correction. She told me that Risa hadn't travelled to Switzerland to be euthanized. She had been unable to travel. No: she had hired some men to steal into her apartment in the middle of the night and kill her. She was found the following morning with a plastic bag over her head. Or so I was told.

A Letter from Anna to Risa
December 23, 1948*

Dearest Risa,

I just got your letter of December 14th. It made me so sad that I couldn't even cry. And then I thought that tomorrow it will be 1949 years that a baby was born in Bethlehem — who was destined to save mankind. His birth, however, didn't save anybody — but His death on the cross was a fulfilment of his mission. I thought about this paradox — and I still couldn't cry. And then, looking for something among my notes, my eyes happened to fall on a poem by Swinburne and all of a sudden I could cry — and after that I felt a lot better. Because if you cry about things — you still have hope, deep down in your heart. Some kind of hope. Even if it's the decadent hope of a great, philosophic brain, who stopped believing in his life mission like Nietzsche: "Wem das Leben misslungen ist, der sehe zu, dass ihm das Sterben

---

* Written shortly after Risa received confirmation that Max, her husband, had been transported to Majdanek in 1943 (presumed dead in transit). Though Anna and Risa would most naturally have communicated in German, their native tongue, and indeed usually wrote to each other in that language, this letter is in English and appears to have been stamped by an Austrian censor. In 1948, Risa lived in the state of Lower Austria, in the town of Pernitz. Between April 27, 1945, and July 27, 1955, Lower Austria was part of the Soviet zone of Allied-occupied Austria. English was Anna's fourth or fifth language. I have not corrected any errors of grammar in fidelity to the original.

gelinge … " (As if death could.)[*] Once you stop crying for the people you loved and lost, for the things you never had and always wanted — when you arrive at this point, you are not really alive anymore: That is the point, when you let yourself die. Like the men in the K.Z.[†] (as Frankl describes it in his book)[‡] — once they smoked their last cigarette instead of trading it for a bit of soup, which might have saved them starving to death — they were actually through with life.

Maybe it's foolish to copy poetry in a letter which has to travel 3000 miles[§] — but I've done so many foolish things in my life and those I regretted doing were the sensible and logical ones, so here goes:[¶]

> I am tired of tears and laughter,
>   And men that laugh and weep;
> Of what may come hereafter
>   For men that sow to reap:
> I am weary of days and hours,
> Blown buds of barren flowers,
> Desires and dreams and powers

---

* This appears to be a paraphrase of a line from *Thus Spake Zarathustra*. The original reads: "*Manchem missräth das Leben: ein Giftwurm frisst sich ihm an's Herz. So möge er zusehn, dass ihm das Sterben um so mehr gerathe.*" ("To many men life is a failure; a poison-worm gnaweth at their heart. Then let them see to it that their dying is all the more a success.") The translation of Anna's line is "Let him who has failed in life see to it that he succeeds in dying."

† Also abbreviated K.L., *Konzentrationslager* (concentration camp).

‡ Viktor Frankl, psychiatrist and Holocaust survivor (1905–1997).

§ Anna is writing from her home in Notre-Dame-de-Grâce, Montreal.

¶ The poem is "The Garden of Proserpine," by Algernon Charles Swinburne (1866). Anna quotes only part of the poem.

And everything but sleep.
There go the loves that wither,
The old loves with wearier wings;
And all dead years draw thither,
And all disastrous things;
Dead dreams of days forsaken,
Blind buds that snows have shaken,
Wild leaves that winds have taken,
Red strays of ruined springs.

We are not sure of sorrow,
And joy was never sure;
To-day will die to-morrow;
Time stoops to no man's lure;
And love, grown faint and fretful,
With lips but half regretful
Sighs, and with eyes forgetful
Weeps that no loves endure.

From too much love of living,
From hope and fear set free,
We thank with brief thanksgiving
Whatever gods may be
That no life lives for ever;
That dead men rise up never;
That even the weariest river
Winds somewhere safe to sea.

I wasn't surprised that Frankl was not of much help to you. I was afraid of that: Talented people are egocentric, they have to be, otherwise they couldn't accomplish anything. I'm glad you met this young doctor in Innsbruck, but you must realize by now that if you yourself are so little interested in a certain Risa Seidner-Weiser* that you let her die — inch by inch — no doctor can do anything. It is your own mind, your own emotions which are killing your otherwise normal body. Does this sound very cruel to you? But I have to say it — if it goes on like that — I might soon not have another chance of telling you anything at all: If I mourn for my brother, I have at least one comfort: for him, life in itself, was too precious a thing to be willfully destroyed, no matter what sufferings, physical and emotional, he had to endure.

You seem to hate yourself much more than Hitler hated any Jew — you are punishing yourself just as cruelly as any SS man could. And just as them, you punish for crimes never committed. You feel guilty to be still alive while Maxi has been dead for such a long time. But can't you understand that Maxi's mind and soul could come alive — partly at least — if those who loved him would be really alive? If they would be sufficiently alive to build some kind of monument to his name and memory — it isn't a monument in stone or marble which keeps memory alive, it is thoughts and deeds. And why not do your share that history should never repeat itself again? How many Maxis do you think could have been saved if Christians like you would not have decided that they rather die together with the Jews

* This is Risa's married name. Max and Anna shared the surname Seidner from their father. Weiser was their mother's maiden name, and also the name proudly associated with the Wiener Sprachschule (the language school), founded by Carl Weiser.

than educate their fellow Christians to a saner attitude? Because murder only begets murder and defeatism defeat. One year ago 700,000 Jews were threatened by unnumbered millions of Arabs.* It would have been easy for them to let themselves die together with the only hope for the remaining 12,000,000 Jews all over the world. Did they do it? If anywhere a miracle was performed in modern times — it certainly was here. A little crowd opposed by millions of savage enemies, betrayed by their friends and allies to the point of infamy. Did they use it as an alibi for suicide? I never thought that I'll ever find the world worthy of the sacrifice of our 6,000,000 Dead and Tortured. But they produced the miracle of Israel. Because each man in Palestine was not alone — behind each Israeli soldier stood and stands the shadows of 600 men and women, crying out to him that there is no retreat for a Jew and if he falls without accomplishing his life mission, 600 of them will stay unrevenged and uselessly sacrificed. And do you know how many Christians are fighting alongside the Jews in Palestine? Not only because they believe in Israel's right, but because it is the only constructive way of expiating their collective sin. I could name you some English aristocrats who worked in the Jewish Underground in Palestine, while the British were still there, I could name others British or American who never

* The following remarks about Israel and Arab peoples are anathema to me. But I reproduce them here so as not to shade Anna's remarks with my bias.

stopped fighting for the rights of Israel, even if they did not use other weapons than public speech and the written word....*

Would you really like to hear again about how we live here? Put down in black and white, our lives seem very drab and commonplace — the mad scramble every morning around 7 o'clock to get the working and studying part of the family out of the house. The bellow of a radio, put on too loud by a hand still drugged by sleep. The weather report which decides whether my next two hours will be spent in worrying anxiously (whether Genek† and Jettka didn't get stuck in snow banks or skidded with the car on slippery roads) or whether I'll be able to concentrate on what I have to do this particular morning. If the weather is exceptionally bad and the radio announcer warns everybody off the roads who doesn't have to be out, I'll worry about Ada going to school by bus (about 1 hour) and Eva who has to walk 15 minutes to school. But there are also those rare days, when the sun shines like in Davos, the air is crisp and invigorating — and the city has sanded properly the roads. I feel young and carefree and start thinking about which work should be tackled first. From 9 to 4, on weekdays, I don't worry about housework (for the last few years) — there is a white-haired angel with a motherly face, who takes care of the

* I have excised a short paragraph containing an aside about Anna's sister, Henrietta (also known as Jetka or Jettka), which is unrelated to the rest of the letter.

† Pet name for Eugene, Anna's husband.

house for me in these hours. And so while Genek supervises construction jobs,* visits clients or does other things which usually are known to "bring home the bacon," while Jetka works around her desk, day in, day out, to co-ordinate his efforts and put them on record, budgeting and distributing the income of the business, while they are on the "putting in" side, I'm now purely on the "taking out" side. Like all individuals, who live on the sweat and work of others, I'm a very useful person to have around: they would have an awfully hard time to spend all the money they earn in such a graceful way, if I wouldn't be here. Besides, who would know that Gene is a successful engineer and businessman if his wife wouldn't be very active in social work, seen, all dressed up in shabby coat and hat, working hard at straightening out bewildered newcomers from the D.P. camps in Europe, taking them to hospital clinics for medical check-ups, riding in taxi cabs to parts of the city — you wouldn't think they can happen on this continent.† Well, evenings again, I put on some make up on my face to cover up the tears I cried during the day, I pull my mouth into an understanding smile for the idle rich and I go to meetings and social gatherings, I pray in good English, I read the handwritings of nice people

* Eugene was an engineer by training. After immigrating to Montreal, he founded a cement construction company. He hired Anna's sister, Jetka, to do his bookkeeping.

† After settling in Canada, Anna and Eugene spent the rest of their lives helping refugees — mostly Jews who had survived the Holocaust — come to Canada, find work, and integrate.

trying to find out why they can't be happy* — and by the time I go to bed at 1 or 1/2 past one, at night, I am too tired to see any sense in any of it. What I really would like to do would be going back to university, getting a degree, becoming a professional of some kind, instead of being "voluntarily" ten different things. Voluntary social worker, honorary vice-president, secretary and editor of a news bulletin — all this doesn't make up for that if somebody asks what I am? I have a very hard time to give a straight answer. Only my D.P.s don't ask me what I really am, they are so glad I exist. As a very young girl I always dreamt of being loved just as I am — everybody then seemed to want to change me over. Now, it came to pass — but I am too old. Somebody will call me up "because he or she just wants to hear my voice to feel better for the rest of the day," another will drive quite a distance in cold weather to see the "Madonna" who wipes your tears away with a joke. It is wonderful, but it still makes me cry, not happy. And I always thought that being loved like that must make you very happy. Neither do I get it for nothing. There are many hours of study behind knowing what to say over the telephone, if somebody is blue and depressed, what joke to use and when — and first and foremost to camouflage real help under joking friendship: To talk and write for people who don't know the

* As indicated below, Anna spent much of her time in the '40s as a voluntary social worker, helping people in person and remotely.

language of their new country, to lessen the hurt and the shock when they find out how few people really care what happened to the refugees from the Hitler hell. To interpret the new country to them in European terms, to make their reactions understandable to the people here — come to think of it, I'm not such a "Nichtstuer"* after all. But if I succeed in performing some "linguistic" achievement — I pause a little and think of our brother Maxi. I think that he would have liked it, that he is glad and proud that a bit of his work is carried on: "Non omnis moriar ..."†

And then I cry a bit and wish I would be a good writer and could dedicate a wonderful novel to the memory of my brother, an important contribution to the psychology of our times ... But like the "Jongleur de Notre Dame" I can dedicate to him only small deeds of kindness, a little speech held here and there and numberless letters written in four different languages.

I had hoped that you will get well and that you will carry on his work. You could, you know. You have the same training and the same interests. But tragically — you prefer to die than make his spirit live.

I hope that none of my D.P.s ever reads my letter to you: doesn't seem much of a madonna writing such a cruel letter to a sister-in-law, I profess to love. But I'm so terribly disappointed:

---

* A layabout.

† "Not all of me will die." Horace.

I always hoped that you will get better, after all you're young, I think a year or two younger than me (and I think I might still achieve something). That you will pick up and carry on yours and Maxi's life work working at the things you were both interested in. I hoped that you will remarry some day and be and have a companion. You see, I honestly believe that Maxi wouldn't mind, that is his spirit, which is alive, his body and his bodily emotions are gone they have no validity any longer. You know how crazily jealous I always was of Genek — I still wouldn't like him to love another woman as long as I'm around, but if I'm gone, I want him to take another companion for himself and another mother for the family. I would also want somebody to carry on the work I'm doing, I would want to dedicate achievements to my memory. I do believe in the immortality of the spirit and I think that the best way to honor our dead is to live not to die.

I don't even know whether you are well enough to read this very long and involved letter. But it is my way of saying good bye to you, my hopes connected with you and everything else I used to love in Vienna.

Just the same, try to get better Darling.

With love from all of us Hania*

* Anna's pet name.

V

It has been ten years since I visited Marta in Vienna.

In the autumn of 2020, an amendment to the Austrian Citizenship Act came into effect. It declared that victims of Nazi persecution in Austria and their descendants could obtain (or regain) citizenship. When I told my father, he was immediately interested. He has passed down to me a fondness for Europe that I suspect is not shared by the rest of my immediate family. To apply, we needed to prove our filiation and our relationship to my grandmother, Eva. We needed to obtain background checks. We needed to prove that Eva herself had never been convicted of a crime. I could tell that she was uncomfortable with all of this; and it was whispered that her sister, Ada, could not understand why we would want such a thing. Who would want to become a citizen of a country that would have killed you less than a century ago? It was and remains a good point. But I am selfish: I wanted to live in Europe, and this was my ticket. Within five months, I was a citizen. I am told that, until the age of thirty-five, I can only live in Austria under the condition that I perform national service in the military that, eighty-five years ago, began systematically to displace and then murder my family. But I am a citizen now. These are my crimes, too, now.

I live in Paris, thanks to the freedom of movement granted by the European Union, near the canal, with my cat. Last weekend my girlfriend and I visited Vienna for my birthday. It was a world apart, because I am a world apart; I am no longer young in the way I was then; I am in love; I have real thoughts of a concrete future. We visited two of the addresses where Eugene, Anna, Ada, and Eva might have lived — the number is known, but the exact street is ambiguous. One stands on Linke Wienzeile, the other on Mariahilferstrasse, ten minutes away by foot. For the first time I

couldn't imagine anyone from those years emerging from these buildings.

It was my first time in Vienna since meeting Marta. I thought to contact her but didn't. I could well have met her for the purposes of writing this story, described the lines that have no doubt grown deeper upon her face, the kindness that no doubt still lingers in her smile. We could well have retraced our steps and struggled to recall, together, everything we did a decade ago. She may well have a memory better than my own; I would have done well to exploit it.

But I can't. Some memories are better left undisturbed. To rewrite them now, as I have been doing, only distorts them. To revisit them with Marta would have distorted them further. Every history says more about the present in which it is written than the past about which it is written. And I am tired of this present. I have had to shake the snow globe to let the glitter fall. But consider it shaken; I will not come again.

Chapter 3

The One About the Rabbi

Once an angry man dragged his father along the ground through his own orchard. "Stop!" cried the groaning old man at last, "Stop! I did not drag my father beyond this tree."

— Gertrude Stein, *The Making of Americans*

I

I first looked at the dead when I was eleven years old. The ghastly dead in black and white, rag and bone, piled in heaps beside mass graves, spilling out of wheelbarrows, mouths agape, sightless eyes like spheres of smoked glass. They have haunted me since and will do so forever. They were daughters, sons, mothers, fathers — people with names and desires, occupations, sins, accomplishments, doubts. And they were murdered, a fact so plain and brutal that a photograph can hardly represent it.

Before I looked at them, I was told about them; before I knew about literature, about geography, about arithmetic, about the history of my own country, I knew about the Holocaust.

I remember, in sixth grade, sitting at the back of the classroom on the third floor of the Jewish People's and Peretz School (or JPPS), on rue Van Horne, staring once again at the blown-up images that had become more familiar to me than the photographic image of my own face, as the teacher moved from slide to slide on the school's newly acquired SMART Board. On this late afternoon, in early April, with the classroom windows opened for the first time in months and the outdoors beckoning, we weren't learning about the Holocaust per se, as we had many times before, but about something called The March of the Living. I knew about "the March," as it was called, because my eldest brother Max was about to board a plane to be a part of it. We twelve-year-olds were being awakened to a holy experience that we could one day expect to have for ourselves. We spoke about the March, almost in hushed tones, and those of us with siblings who had attended or were about to attend mentioned this fact often and proudly.

Max was about to fly very far away indeed. One week in Poland, where, along with thousands of other high schoolers from over fifty countries, he would visit Warsaw and Kraków, seeking the traces of a once vibrant Jewish community. He would spend long hours on buses cutting into the dark forests and fields that surrounded the most infamous camps: Auschwitz-Birkenau, Majdanek, Treblinka. He would stand before the mass graves into which small Polish towns once expelled and condemned their Jewish populations. And then … and then he would fly to Israel, where finally he would *see*, he would *understand*. The land of Our People. Our Safe Haven. The Eretz. One day, I, too, would see and understand. I would travel thousands of miles and into the darkness, before emerging into light.

The slideshow ends. The bell rings. We spill out of the school doors like ants toward the bus stops and carpool lanes.

II

In Basel, in the year 1903, the young Marxist Dov Ber Borochov was one of nearly two hundred delegates at the Sixth Zionist Congress to oppose the "Uganda Scheme," backed by Theodor Herzl and his ally, British colonial secretary Joseph Chamberlain. The idea was to encourage the migration of about a million European Jews to a tract of arable land in what is now Kenya, either as a second-best alternative to the settlement of Jews in Palestine (considered the true Jewish homeland by Zionists), or as a proof of concept for the eventual establishment of a Jewish state there — in either case, the Jews of Uganda were to have a high degree of local autonomy and religious freedoms. Herzl, impatient by temperament, had become even more so following the Kishinev pogrom in Bessarabia a few months prior, and he arrived at the congress insistent on pushing the plan to the centre of the agenda. There was, so Herzl had contended in his pamphlet *Der Judenstaat* seven years prior, no true safe haven for Jews in the Diaspora; one had to be *made* — with money, statecraft, and force if necessary.

The British interest in the Uganda plan was mostly self-motivated. In 1893, the British Imperial East Africa Company had been in dire straits, facing financial collapse, an inability to secure investment, and crumbling infrastructure, after only five years of administering its 639,000 square kilometres of territory (comprising present-day Somalia and Kenya). The BIEAC was consequently handed over to the British government, which fared little better at administration, ill-advisedly sinking over £5 million into the Uganda Railway, a move that was meant to bring the riches of the East African interior into imperial possession, but which ultimately and dramatically underperformed as an enterprise. Funnelling Jewish investment into the area — as well as able bodies — was suddenly a very bright idea. Even better, Uganda could be used to reduce the pressure then being placed on the British Empire by the influx of Jewish refugees fleeing pogroms in Eastern Europe. The British were discovering a logic that many of Europe's most powerful states would come to adopt vis-à-vis Zionism. Call it a coincidence of wants: the powers that be wanted the Jews to go anywhere but *here*; Zionists wanted the Jews to go nowhere but *there*. Zionism represented a tidy deal for everyone from the mild-mannered race purist to the rabid antisemite. Herzl, ever the pragmatist, sought the audience of both and everyone in between.

Opposition to Uganda at the congress came in various shades. Most dissenters agreed, at base, that a homeland in Palestine, specifically, should not be compromised, no matter how difficult it might be to bring about. Borochov was one such voice. But he disagreed with Herzl on more fundamental, philosophical grounds as well. Herzl was, to his mind, a bourgeois capitalist and opportunist whose idea of Zionism, if put into practice, would squander the role that the Jewish people had to play in the fusion of socialism and nationalism. Herzl appealed to autocrats (the kaiser, the sultan, the queen of England) and to rapacious bankers (the Rothschilds, Samuel Montagu, Maurice de Hirsch) to effect by force what should be brought about organically, by the people. In effect, what Herzl offered these notables was a continuation of the various colonial enterprises they operated and profited from. He put it clearly in *Der Judenstaat*, writing that a Zionist state in Palestine would "form a part of a wall of defense for Europe in Asia, an outpost of civilization against barbarism." This was a promise to continue a form of social and economic exploitation that any good socialist should abhor.

Borochov, born in 1881 to a household of teachers in the town of Zolotonosha, believed that European Jewry maintained an "inverted pyramid" relationship to class: a small minority were labourers; the majority occupied the professional classes. On the whole, they had been cheated of the natural social development that, according to the law of dialectical materialism, should have been their due. The only solution was to right the pyramid — to reform Jewish society from the bottom up, restoring to Jewish men and women the roles of producers and labourers that had mostly been denied them by gentiles who had pigeonholed their kind into specific professional occupations (only to recurrently use their professional status against them). But this socialist dream could be achieved only if the Jewish people were given the opportunity to begin from scratch, without the interference of gentile society — to till and sow their own soil and build their own towns and cities. The nation needed a state, in other words. And the state should be located in the homeland from which the Jews had been in exile for thousands of years. This was how Borochov saw it.

Neither Herzl nor Borochov, it should be said, thought much about the problem of what to do with all the people who already lived in Palestine. Each professed his preferred genre of ethnic cleansing: Herzl famously imagined something like a G-rated version of what would actually come to pass and be known as the Nakba:

> We must expropriate gently the private property on the estates assigned to us. We shall try to spirit the penniless population across the border by procuring employment for it in the transit countries, while denying it employment in our own country. The property owners will come over to our side. Both the process of expropriation and the removal of the poor must be carried out discreetly and circumspectly.

Borochov had less time for practicalities and more romantic feeling for "the poor." To his credit, he never imagined forcibly expelling or expropriating the Palestinians; he even thought that the Jew and the Arab could work harmoniously, side-by-side, as a single proletariat. But for all that, he insisted that there would be only one dominant culture, the Jewish one, because the Jews would be the ones to bring enlightenment to those lands, order to those societies. They would make the desert bloom, as the saying goes, and it would be to *their* culture that everyone on the land would assimilate:

> The natives of the Land of Israel will assimilate economically and culturally with whoever brings order to the country, whoever undertakes the development of the forces of production of the Land of Israel. It is the Jewish immigrants who will undertake the development of the forces of production [there] and the local population … will soon assimilate economically and culturally to the Jews.

In any case, as we now know, some combination of these distinct visions would ultimately obtain in reality. In the interwar period, per the historian Rashid Khalidi, "a separate Jewish-controlled sector of the economy was created through the exclusion of Arab labour from Jewish-owned firms under the slogan of 'Avoda ivrit,' Hebrew labour, and the injection of truly massive amounts of capital from abroad." A few years later, in 1948, 750,000 Palestinians would be forced from their lands, flee in panic and in fear for their lives, and, in the subsequent few years, be denied any right to return to their homes or claim restitution for their stolen property — all in the push to establish a Jewish state. Those who remained would either be killed or, more commonly, "assimilated" as Israelis (many Arab Israelis would say that proper assimilation was never achieved;

most have experienced the psychological torments of xenophobia for decades). And yet the fledgling nation would, for a relatively long time, be run by self-proclaimed socialists, and would build its reputation atop the archipelago of small labour communes that had begun dotting the landscape under the British Mandate and the various armed militias that were set up to protect them (these would, by and large, eventually be merged to form the Israeli Defense Forces).

This Labour Zionism was the natural and inevitable outgrowth of Jewish European culture. When the Jewish Labour Bund rejected Zionism in 1901 — on the grounds that it represented a sort of surrender of the rights that belonged to workers everywhere, no matter the territory, to the forces of production that they employed, as well as a misunderstanding of Jewish nationhood as residing "over there," rather than in Jewish culture and traditions long established "right here" in Europe — it was only a matter of time before a Zionist faction splintered off. The Poale Zion (or Workers of Zion) championed just such a merger of nationalist and socialist principles, following the theories laid out by Borochov and others. Appealing both to the politics and the fearful vigilance of Jewish people worldwide, the group spawned dozens of local offshoots across Europe and North America, promulgating the socialist utopia that would finally give a home to this scattered people.

One such group, having grown influential among Jewish immigrants in Canada and the United States, set out to educate a new generation of Labour Zionists in the mould of the Poale. In 1909, Russian-born Chaim Zhitlowsky, one of the movement's chief advocates, argued in the pages of his New York–based, Yiddish-language magazine that the Poale Zion should establish Yiddish secular pedagogy across America. His readers would not have been surprised: Yiddish had long been at the core of socialist notions of Jewish culture and nationhood. In opposition to the

Herzlian, Political-Zionist idea of reviving Hebrew as the Jewish vernacular, the Bund and associated organizations emphasized the *actual* centrality of Yiddish to European Jewish life, considering it a folk language of the common people. As Zhitlowsky understood, Yiddish would give perfect expression to the fusion of socialism and Jewish nationalism that the Poale was endeavouring to achieve. And North America, where Yiddish could be picked up in this sense without the interference of any of its socio-historical baggage, was the ideal laboratory for his experiment.

At the 1910 Convention of the Poale Zion Party in Montreal, it was resolved that secular schools teaching socialism, popular Jewish history, and the Yiddish language should be established across America. The first one appeared in New York that year. Three years later, in 1913, members of the Poale Zion in Montreal founded the National Radical School in Mile End. It began as a supplementary school only, but from its inception it exerted a considerable secular counterforce to the incumbent Talmud Torah schools, which championed tradition and religiosity. Factionalism quickly germinated. In 1914, the National Radical School splintered, with a new faction arguing that Hebrew need not be subordinated to Yiddish as a national, secular language for the Jews, and that young Jewish students should be given an education in Jewish religion, albeit from a cultural (rather than theological) perspective.

The original National Radical School became known, in 1918, as the Jewish Peretz School, named for Polish writer and playwright I.L. Peretz. The splinter group declared itself the Yidishe Folkshule, or the Jewish People's School, and soon occupied a building on Saint-Urbain. The Poale Zion funded both of them for a few years, before backing the Folkshule exclusively, allowing the latter to develop into a proper day school, the first of its kind in Montreal since the establishment of the Talmud Torah. Both schools would move locations multiple times over the decades. And by 1971, both would find themselves in financial trouble. They merged as the Jewish People's and Peretz School, or JPPS, the school my parents, my brothers, and I attended in turn. They also formed a secondary school, named for poet Chaim Nahman Bialik.

But by then they had long ceased to be what they once were. For my cohort, attending in the early 2000s, there would be no socialist education — no readings of Marx or Rosa Luxemburg, no people's history of Yiddish or world Jewry. What Yiddish instruction remained would be but a shadow of its original purpose; what snatches of the language I would learn would mostly be the lyrics to songs about the Holocaust. The "Labour" element of Labour Zionism had withered away, just as it had been withering before the last breath of Yitzhak Rabin in Israel. There would be no poalim or poalot among us, only the children of businesspeople, lawyers, and doctors (someone's idea of a Jewish joke). And they would be destined to the same fates as their parents — but not before a few years in the back of a classroom, with May coming on, watching the dead appear and disappear among the slides.

III

When I say that JPPS and Bialik were, when I attended, "no longer what they once were," I mean less that they had become something else than that they almost ceased to be anything resembling a school altogether.

In fact, I don't have much to say about my experience at JPPS. It was elementary school — grades 1–6 in Quebec — and there wasn't much at stake. I learned what I needed to learn, was treated kindly by all my teachers, made some friends, shared my first kiss, played in the snow, and stared out the window all within the chain-link fence that ran the school's perimeter. My dad recently told me that, in his final year there, he had a British history teacher who, deciding that her subject matter was too imperial, threw out the curriculum and taught her students about the Cuban Revolution instead. There were posters of Mao and Che Guevara on the walls. I had no such excitement and no such stories to tell.

When I moved to Bialik — grades 7–11 (or ages thirteen to seventeen) — I learned for the first time what it meant to attend an institution that was missing a guiding spirit, like flying thirty thousand feet in a plane that has just had its engines cut, coasting on the wind, slowly falling. Most things worked fine. The floors were buffed each morning and the (garishly painted) walls cleaned. Classes ran on time, the library (I think) had a good variety of books, and the students mostly wore their uniforms as directed.

What jarred were the people. There was no accounting for the heterogeneous group of teachers and administrators who worked there. A handful of instructors held Ph.D.s, while some others were famously incapable of answering questions regarding the coursework they were responsible for teaching. I had a calculus instructor who seemed to be taking the calculus course she was teaching at night school, concurrently with her course. (I really liked her, for the record. She would exclaim, "I'm not there yet!" whenever someone asked a question pertaining to material covered in a future chapter.) I had a Hebrew teacher who, on the first day of class, told us all in no uncertain terms that we would be receiving 72 percent (i.e., Cs) no matter how hard we worked or how well-behaved we were. (I don't know about my peers, but I finished the class with a 72 percent.) I had a physics teacher who had so many phobias, probably induced in him from years of bullying at the hands of cruel students, that he seemed to dread lab work more than we did. (He once kicked me out of class for saying "don't worry, man" to another student, explaining, "I hate that word. Don't ever say that word," by which he presumably meant the word "man.") I had a Jewish history teacher who gave me and my friends an A on our creative assignment — a rap about Uriel da Costa — despite never having listened to it. (When it was time to play it to the class, after the grade had been assigned, he said, "Wow, that's actually good!") I had an English teacher who taught an entire generation of students that the only way to read literature was as Freudian psychoanalysts — straight lines represented the superego, the sea was the id, triangles recalled the Oedipus complex, vegetables being cut in the kitchen symbolized the castration complex, and so forth. (She was well-meaning.)

I had a PE teacher who was infamous for his outbursts: he called a Sephardic friend of mine a "terrorist" during a pickup basketball game; he threw volleyballs in frustration at several students; he frequently blew his whistle to pause whatever game we were playing in order to relate the dynamics of a given play to a scene in the Old Testament; he referred to the students in the *section française* (children of immigrants who, by Quebec law, were not allowed to receive any anglophone instruction) as "stray cats" and frequently shooed them off the basketball court and into the weightlifting room; once, seeing a group of us gathered outside to cool off after a sweaty session of floor hockey or the like, he asked in stupefaction, "What are you, a bunch of homos?"; someone I know claims, with some good evidence in my opinion, that this teacher stole his tefillin for about a year.* (This same teacher once tried to sell me a pair of used gold-coloured Nikes from the trunk of his car.) Despite all this, he was an amusing and undoubtedly creative guy: he invented several sports, including vodgeky (a combination of volleyball, dodgeball, and hockey), flickerball (a combination of American football and basketball), and lead-up rugby (effectively Irish football). I had a biology teacher who gave me a completely undeserved A because

* Tefillin are a set of leather boxes containing scrolls of parchment with verses from the Torah, or the Hebrew Bible, inscribed on them. They are worn by Jewish men (affixed to the head and arms via leather straps) for morning prayer.

I once brought in an old copy of *Gray's Anatomy* belonging to my parents to show the class. I had a substitute Hebrew teacher (a retired former Hebrew teacher, filling in for his wife) who, in an effort to discipline a couple of unruly back-of-the-class chatters, said, "You know, I used to interrogate terrorists in Lebanon. I know some techniques that would shut you up for good." Being in the top Yiddish class, I had the privilege of automatically getting placed in the Yiddish choir, despite having no vocal talent. (Ninety-five percent of this choir was completely tune- and pitch-less; despite this, it once performed a slate of Holocaust songs in front of the mayor of Montreal, and had to watch the horror slowly grip his face as the clamorous, dysphonic, postmodern noise it produced threatened to disfigure the stately rotunda of city hall.) And what Yiddish instruction we had was from curricula designed decades prior; our exercise sheets were a *mise-en-abyme* of photocopies of photocopies of photocopies of the same sheets our parents would have used (a fitting image for a place so frozen in time). We had five principals in the five years I attended (one of whom should have thought twice about going into high school education with the surname "Butman").

And yet the students were arguably the greater producers of chaos. We were unruly as a rule. One could leave class for the bathroom and return forty minutes later without so much as a comment from the teacher. Students heckled instructors (especially substitutes) over mundane gaffes. They pranked teachers regularly. (One such joke involved placing a walkie talkie in the ceiling panels of the physics classroom and, while the instructor was grading papers alone, announcing from the heavens: "Mr. ____, this is God speaking. Repent ...") Some bad behaviour was, to be fair, stereotypical: kids selling weed from their lockers, performing sex acts in the elevator (or in the single-use bathrooms, or discreetly in class beneath a desk), cheating on provincial exams, brandishing butterfly knives to assert their dominance. But whatever was stereotypical was least tolerated — all of these incidents were dealt with swiftly, hushed up and tidied away. If, however, you wanted to disrupt class by chanting old sailor tunes at the top of your lungs, or spend an entire lesson playing multiplayer RPGs on your school-provided laptop, or abstain from doing an assignment on the grounds that it sounded stupid, you met little resistance other than the bemused (or infuriated) reply from an instructor who could usually give it just as good as they got it.

If the foregoing reads like a round of uncalled-for potshots being levelled against a decent, harmless Jewish day-school filled with well-meaning staff, I can only say that I haven't gotten to the nefarious part, yet. All this bedlam would be completely understandable, even charming, if it weren't the foil for a relatively effective and persistent campaign of pedagogical propaganda — a system of manufactured consent for the unassuming youth. Let me tell you another story: At fourteen years old, I was kicked out of Hebrew class for attempting to present on the casualties of Operation Cast Lead (Israel's three-week campaign against Hamas and invasion of Gaza from 2008 to 2009). The assignment was to elaborate, in Hebrew, on a news item relating to Israel. I got no further than showing the title slide, featuring a photograph of a crowd of Palestinian civilians hoisting a body draped in the Palestinian flag, before Mrs. R. began to wave her arms at me, saying with the gravelly tones of a lifelong smoker, "No, no no, get out, Libman. Out. Not funny. Out."

So I went out. I did think it was funny, at the time. And lest I should pretend now to have been a righteous objector then, I want to be clear that I *had known* that Mrs. R. would take exception to my choice of subject matter, and that I'd be kicked out of class. That was the point. I was a smartass. If there was any part of me that felt apathy toward Israel, and even empathy toward the Palestinians, it was the part that looked up to my older brother,

Max, who was on his way to university to study history, and who had explained to me that Israel, contrary to everything I had been told, was no angel — that it was even the perpetrator of immoral actions. I might not yet have felt indignant knowing that fact; but I felt *cool* knowing it, being unique among a student population that, as a rule, considered such ideas to be anathema to Jewish culture and antisemitic, full-stop.

Nearly every school, of course, serves as a funnel for filling young heads with state propaganda. But how many of them perform such a service for a foreign state? I've known the Israeli national anthem, by heart, for as long as I've known the Canadian one. We sang it at school assemblies; we sang it during moments of silence on Yom HaZikaron, the official remembrance day in Israel; we sang it in Nathan Phillips Square, after being bussed there in droves for participation in the yearly Israeli Independence Day rally. (I remember gawking at the ranks of counterprotestors, anti-Zionist Haredim, and being told by peers and teachers that they weren't real Jews.) It was a common occurrence to see an Israeli flag in the halls of Bialik, or a map of Israel pinned to a classroom wall. I can't recall ever seeing the Canadian flag, or a map of Quebec or of Montreal. Almost all of us students visited Israel as part of some high-school fellowship or another. Almost all of our Hebrew teachers had been born and raised in Israel and would not hear a word against it. Needless to say, any reference to Palestinian lives that didn't include the qualifiers *enemy*, *barbaric*, *savage*, *antisemitic*, *genocidal*, *uncooperative*, *corrupt*, and the like, was verboten in the classroom or in public speech settings. Mostly, though, you didn't mention Palestinians at all.

I'd love to say that this conformity was administered with a heavy hand — then, at least, an observer could begin to sympathize with us. But our ideological bubble was so perfectly sealed, and it so perfectly refracted any contradictory information from without, that it harboured hardly any internal friction at all. That is why the exceptions, like being booted from class, are so memorable to me. In Jewish history class, we were once assigned the task of determining whether each of us felt most like a Montrealer, a Quebecker, a Canadian, or a Jew. (That's right.) When I stated my case as a proud Montrealer, Mr. C. pushed back, asking if I *really* felt more like a Montrealer than a Jew. After all, at the last instance, when it *really* came down to it, who would remain to accept me?

Contemporary Jewish life is shot through with such ironies. We rightly claim it to be antisemitic when others accuse us of dual or foreign allegiances, or when others assume that because we are Jewish we must hate Palestinians. But then we turn right around and teach our children that, despite being Canadians, they must love the State of Israel as their homeland. (I once polled several of my classmates as to whether they'd sooner support Canada or Israel if either were to come under attack. You can guess, now, at the response.) And we encourage the conflation of Judaism and Zionism ourselves, and therefore the idea that a two-state solution is an improbability, and a one-state solution a demographic time bomb. We demand to be judged by the content of our character and not by our religion, and yet we resist the idea of assimilation — even a pluralistic assimilation — outright. We cling so conspicuously to a narrative of exceptionality and yet we love to nurture the chip on our shoulder whenever someone decides to notice the exception. The problem is not that we don't assimilate, or that we do it too well. It's that we fall prey to such profound hypocrisies.

The result, for me, was a long childhood of indoctrination (some of it passive, and some of it, if such a thing is possible, even well-intentioned), of which I was only faintly aware, followed by a violent, Copernican revolution in my understanding of the world, of the people that inhabited it, and of myself. And as with any good dialectical turn, my moment of truth came during and as the result of my participation in *the* centrepiece of our little world's collective orthodoxy — the experience designed to end all other experiences, to give us all the last word at the green age of seventeen: the March of the Living.

IV

I have been to Israel twice. The second time was incidental. It was the summer after high school graduation, and I had been accepted for a fully funded science research fellowship at the Weizmann Institute. I say it was incidental because the fellowship could have been anywhere in the world. I wanted to do science per se, not be in Israel. That the two would have to go hand in hand was a function of the fact that, as a Jew, I would have a leg up on my application. (That said, most of the program's eighty or so participants, from over ten countries, were non-Jewish.) That being in Israel for a second time would ultimately reacquaint me with a sour taste in my mouth may have contributed to the fact that I promptly started dating my blond-haired, blue-eyed, German, and definitely-not-Jewish co-fellow, whose grandfather had been a card-carrying Nazi, during and after the program. (We broke up soon after.)

My first time in Israel was on the March, which bills itself as "an annual educational program, bringing individuals from around the world to Poland and Israel to study the history of the Holocaust and to examine the roots of prejudice, intolerance and hatred." My parents had to pay a couple of thousand dollars for me to attend. But we'd have to wait to get there. We'd have to earn it, narratively speaking, to build up to it. Almost everyone at Bialik went on the trip. (Two of my closest friends, one of them being my most religious friend, were notable exceptions.) In my ignorance, I had thought that the program involved only a handful of high schools across Canada. In fact, as I would glean while staring out at the sea of Jewish teens flooding the fields of what was once K.L. Auschwitz, I was but one of around ten thousand participants from over fifty countries. (Or so the program's website tells me.) We had to apply to attend ("What does the March mean to me?" and other essays), but no one I know was rejected. We spent the winter and early spring of our senior year in nervous anticipation of the various drips of information we received about the trip as the start date approached: the rough outline of our itinerary (the dates of arrival in Poland and departure for Israel), how we Montreal participants would be divvied up across four or five coach buses, what we should pack, etc. We attended a mandatory prep weekend for the trip on the premises of a Jewish summer camp in the Laurentians, during which we watched *Schindler's List* and heard first-hand testimony of the horrors of the camps from survivors. We received T-shirts with the phrase "I AM MARCHING FOR …" printed on the back, followed by a few empty lines. I waited until the last minute before writing, "STEARNS FAMILY." (Stearns was the surname that Eugene and Anna Sternschuss chose to adopt upon their arrival in North America, figuring that Sternschuss would be too foreign; in fact, they had originally settled on "Sterns," but Eugene then felt that this would mark them out immediately as Jews, and somehow got it into his head that adding an *a* would help.)

I can think of no more important educational experience in the subject of history than to bring students to the remnants of and memorials to humankind's most wicked, debased hours: the camps, the killing fields, the gulags, the slave plantations, the residential schools. Understood *as* a past whose residue persists in the present, these sites of commemoration help us to see the way time can sediment itself in layers. Rather than being opportunities to declare that the past is not really past (a meaningless phrase), these are occasions to reckon with the irreversibility of time, and with the social reformations and acts of atonement we have undertaken to cope with time's arrow. It is a sobering experience to trip over one of the thousands of *Stolpersteine* ("stumbling stones") around Berlin — not only because they call to mind the crimes of the past, but also because they call one's attention to the very state that both committed those crimes and, in the present, laid down those stones. This kind of historical thinking, seeing the layering of time within a given space, characterizes the best of our pedagogical experiences. I have been on one or two trips like this. But the March was not one of them.

What was so wrong about the March? Maybe "wrong" is the wrong word; in one sense, in its peculiarity, it was utterly *right*, serving its specific end with tremendous effect. To understand why so many North American Jews of my generation support Israel as a rule, no matter the state's depredations, one must understand the March. As my brother put it to me in a recent text, "Holocaust is perpetually yesterday and tomorrow." You could have printed that on the sides of the buses we rode through Warsaw, Kraków, and the Polish landscape. The trip was not an encounter with history first-hand, as might be promised to a score of Swiss retirees booking a two-week excursion to the Peloponnese. It was the performance of an allegory: just as your grandparents went through hell and emerged, battered, into the light, so too will you travel through the dark reaches of Poland and earn your way to the Promised Land. We therefore did not go to Poland as such, but to a simulacrum of Poland with the time dial turned to 1939–45, the antisemitism dial turned to HIGH, and the pixels set to greyscale. (The official photographs of the trip, which were uploaded at the end of each day to the March website and to a Facebook group whose only members were our parents, were mostly monochromatic, for the Poland portion — and turned to full colour once we landed in Israel.) We travelled 6,500 kilometres to play-act some version of the present that, for all we knew, did not correspond to reality. I say "for all we knew" because we were given no opportunity to confirm this fact. On several occasions I was told not to engage with the locals who wanted to know what our trip was about. The trip rabbi told me one evening that most people in the areas we visited were the children and grandchildren of Nazi sympathizers (plausible) and that they still held onto that ideology (unverifiable). We spoke to no Poles, save the tour guides at the various shrines and emblems to Jewish communities past. We visited no Polish cultural institutions. We studied no Polish history. We learned no Polish customs or traditions. I doubt whether all of us could have found Poland on a map, despite literally being there. When one bus driver announced that it would be a four-hour ride from Warsaw to Kraków, one of the passengers said, in genuine astonishment, "Damn, how big *is* this place?" It was like going to the United States and insisting that everything was as it had been during the Civil War. You wore Union flags around your waist, drove from Gettysburg to Antietam Creek, and treated everyone south of the Mason-Dixon with hostility. Poland was our journey into the underworld; all around us were the signs of death and destruction. Auschwitz, Birkenau, Majdanek, Treblinka. Old, unkempt Jewish cemeteries and disused synagogues. Mossed-over mass graves in quiet forests. Even the food was bad — bland, dry, underportioned.

And then I consider our behaviour and wonder whether the locals wouldn't have looked at us side-eyed anyway. Our not really being in Poland, but rather in the "Poland" that suited the narrative we were all enacting, led us, late one weeknight, into an old Jewish synagogue in Kraków. While there, we were exhorted by the trip's rabbi and the other leaders to belt out classic Jewish songs at the tops of our lungs. Dozens of us were sing-shouting DAVID MELECH YISRAEL CHAI CHAI V'KHAYAM ("David, king of Israel, lives and endures ...") in the middle of a Polish residential neighbourhood at 10:00 p.m., as if to say, "We are here! You tried to get rid of us, but here we are!" This kind of behaviour, boorish and inconsiderate from just about any perspective, only made sense — only took on its felt moral virtue — if we understood our surroundings to be something other than what they were; that is, if we imagined ourselves to be in hostile territory, somehow visiting wartime Poland reconstituted in the present, rather than 2012 Poland, European Union Poland, the Poland of schoolchildren who, like us, knew the past not first-hand but by way of what had been passed down to them. The moral cosmology of the March, whose ultimate purpose (in addition to producing some genuine moments of catharsis) was to prove the logical and ethical necessity of the State of Israel, only cohered if we could imagine ourselves as activists, fighting a power that would like to see us gassed or kneeling beside an open pit. We had to overlay reality with a story (a real story, albeit one that had already happened), casting ourselves and entire nations in specific, categorical roles. It was a form of retroactive fantasy or wish fulfillment — *l'esprit de l'escalier* on a collective scale. This is the only way to properly fathom the hundreds of us who marched through the streets of Tarnów on a sunny, weekend market day, singing Zionist songs with the Israeli flag draped over our backs. A rejoinder seventy years in the making. But to whom?

The camps — where, surely, there was no need to drape a more sinister virtual reality over the remains of an actual death factory — presented their own genre of incongruity. I remember the day we arrived at Auschwitz vividly. It was sunny and warm, blue skies stretching out in every direction. How could a place like this exist in anything but the most horrendous of climates? For the first time in my decade-or-so education about the Holocaust, I imagined the prisoners of Auschwitz labouring under the sun, shrieking under the sun, being led into gas chambers and shovelled out of them under the sun, being loaded onto wheelbarrows under the sun, being transported to the crematoria under the sun, praying to our absent God under the sun. I felt ill; it was ill-fitting. Never have I cried so much in my life. Thousands of Israeli flags, blue March jackets, and white caps filled the slopes of the rail ramp at Birkenau. This, too, sat somehow oddly. On a podium far at the front of the crowd, a bronzed, puffy-faced Chaim Topol (of *Fiddler* fame) spoke to us about the lessons of the Holocaust and the singular importance of Israel. Here we were, standing not as victims but, finally, as victors on the grounds of Auschwitz, remembering on behalf of a world that might sooner prefer to forget. A triumph to be sure. But there was something empty about our performance of this upstanding historiographic duty. It was as if, despite standing there, our feet were not truly touching the ground. We were trying to fasten to something that offered us no hooks. I know now that this is the problem of memorialization as such: history as flailing in the dark, as the attempt to re-instantiate that which has already been pulverized into the sands of time. What remains at Auschwitz? Some buildings, some rails and ballasts, some barbed wire, a guard tower or two. What remains at Majdanek? A shocking mound of ashes under a broad, brutalist dome — like a UFO from some future past. All of it was and is unspeaking. Yet we cannot but insist on dialoguing with it, on reanimating it in the present; so that we can remind ourselves, yes, but also so that we can exact our due, which is always too late. Lateness is the tragedy of history.

In truth, Auschwitz now is an eerie, uncanny place. And not only because of what occurred there. The atmosphere is best captured in Jonathan Glazer's film *The Zone of Interest*, which follows a chapter in the life of Rudolf Höss, the camp's infamous commandant who would eventually be hanged outside of its gates, as he and his wife live their lives, raise their children, and grow their vegetables on the other side of the camp's walls. Their existence is a study in meditative compartmentalization: it is not that they do not hear the prisoners' screams, smell the burning bodies, or see the pillars of smoke belched out of the chimney stacks; it is that they assiduously allow these sense data to pass through them without being registered by their consciousnesses. In one scene, Höss expels ash from his nose into the sink as part of his bedtime routine, without any expression of surprise. At the end of the film, as Höss leaves an SS party in Berlin retching from the booze, the viewer is suddenly transported into the gas chambers of Auschwitz in the present day. The camera pans over the concrete walls, where scratch marks are still visible and appear just as I saw them with my own eyes. We see a crematorium and a woman carefully wiping it down with antibacterial spray. Then we are shown the inside of the museum as the cleaning staff buff the floors and clean the glass case displays. The workers pass by the piles of old shoes, shorn hair, and gutted suitcases with their vacuum cleaners and polishers. The effect is one of utter banality: not of evil, but of the past. The past is something we want so badly to keep alive and something we are therefore content to contain, prop up, illuminate, and coerce into speech. But it can only be limp and silent, for it ceased to live the moment it occurred. It evinces the uncanniness of the zombie, the doppelgänger: that which comes twice, that which recurs — though never in the same way.

Holocaust is perpetually yesterday and tomorrow. This could also be the motto for the State of Israel. One thing that dawns on you as you experience the March is that Israel has monopolized Holocaust historiography. This perhaps mundane fact should strike us as strange. The moment the trip clicked for me — by which I mean, the moment I felt the apparatus of the trip and its pedagogy fall away and the hard reality of the world loom before me — occurred during our visit to Buczyna forest, near Zbylitowska Góra in southern Poland. Today, Buczyna is something akin to a regional park: people take strolls and ride bikes through it; they walk their dogs along its paths and feed the ducks in its pond. Between

1942 and 1943, about ten thousand people were murdered and buried in mass graves there. About two-thirds of these were Jewish men, women, and children who were taken there from the nearby Tarnów ghetto, where they had been interned. We learned that the Polish residents of Tarnów helped their Nazi occupiers perform the dirty work, even if only by jeering at the groups of emaciated Jews as they were marched into the woods. We did not learn whether they also helped out when the Germans marched two thousand or so Christian Poles into the forest to be dispatched in the same way. We learned that some of the town's Jews had managed to escape, and that a small number later returned to the town, their home, after the war, only to be killed by their neighbours who had gotten used to their absence. Now, the mass graves are demarcated by blue-painted iron railings. I remember leaning my weight on one of these railings as the rabbi spoke about what had taken place there, and hearing his voice fade away. I stared for a long time at the ground covering what must have been thousands of skulls, vertebrae, femurs, pelvic bones. I felt weak, utterly useless and undeserving of the survival, several generations on, of which those buried without dignity beneath me had been violently reft. Even beneath the tall grass, you could tell that the earth was uneven, as if stuck in undulation. I recalled what the rabbi had said only moments prior: often, the gunshots whose propulsion would tip the bodies into the pit weren't fatal; buried alive, struggling to breathe among the corpses, some of these revenants cried out as loud as they could; it is said that a faint moaning could be heard each night in Tarnów, only a few kilometres away. I was frozen to the railing, feeling for the umpteenth time since arriving in Poland that I could cry. I looked down. At my feet I noticed a plaque. As I read, I was jolted back into "Poland." There were the Hebrew lyrics that open "Hatikvah," the Israeli national anthem: "As long as the Jewish spirit is yearning deep in the heart ..." Beside this was etched a Star of David, and beneath it the coat of arms of the State of Israel.

Why this? Why Israel? This should not be a banal question; it lies at the very heart of what turns an educational trip about the Holocaust into an apologia for Zionism — not the age-old yearning to return to Zion, but precisely the version of Political Zionism embodied by the State of Israel today. Visitors to Buczyna will unfailingly see two or three of the country's flags tied to the railings. Later, when we were walking to the buses, I asked the rabbi why, throughout our entire time in Poland, we had had to speak of Israel whenever we attempted to speak of the Holocaust. He had the kind of lost-for-words expression on his face that meant he didn't even understand how this could *be* a question, like its very premise blew a fuse every time it was pondered. I suspect that many readers will feel that way. Israel figures itself as the "today" astride which the "yesterday" and "tomorrow" of the Holocaust stands. But what, truly, has it got to do with the horrors that befell European Jewry between 1939 and 1945?* What does it mean that a thought has to pass through the medium of the State of Israel before it can reach its terrible object? This is the shape the problem of the March took as it finally dawned on me, there in the forest, walking back to the buses. Staring out the window and waiting for the coach to start, all I could hear was the clicking of the buttons on the dozens of cell phones that had immediately come out the moment we left the site. Had they no respect? Had no one any respect? I asked the girl next to me, on whom I had been crushing hard, to put hers away. She scoffed. I felt suddenly like a captive. Everyone looked forward to Israel, where we would be in two days' time, except me. I felt duped. How is it that no one cared?

---

* If anything, as the Haavara Agreement of 1933 between Nazi Germany and the Jewish Agency makes clear, the idea of funneling Jews into Palestine was one the Nazis were sympathetic to early on.

From then on the March, for me, was doomed to be top heavy. The significance of Poland — both of what we saw and of my epiphany about how we were made to see it — overshadowed and emptied out what, for my friends, was the greatest part of the trip. We arrived in Israel into an explosion of colour. The food was fabulous, the weather perfect, and the trip leaders' disposition suddenly cheerful. This too was "Israel" rather than Israel — no discussion of the occupation, no visits to the West Bank, no lesson on the Nakba, no introduction to the country's internal political turmoil. The agenda for this half of the history trip was to have fun. We floated on the Dead Sea and zigzagged our way through the Jaffa markets. Hot soldiers were conspicuously brought along to various activities for which their skills were probably unnecessary; flirting was encouraged. Even the heartbreaking visit to Yad Vashem, which sits atop Mount Herzl, ended on a note of absolute triumph, as we emerged to a commanding view of Jerusalem and the occupied West Bank. I don't think there is a more moving museum in the world, whatever its objectives. (Certain events are so terrible, so ineffable, that no ideological script can be adequate to them; the Holocaust was a series of such events, and it will always refuse, to some degree, our writing it.) We suffered; now look what we have got. Look at what history wrought for us. It was indeed this tone of inevitability that we were being groomed to adopt for ourselves vis-à-vis the young state, which loved nothing more than to protest of its antiquity. Here the monopoly on memory was at its most robust. Here the Holocaust took its place as an episode in the long Jewish saga that began with Abraham and ended right here, the arc having bent toward justice at last, the return finally complete. *And what now?* you could be forgiven for asking yourself, as you stared into the hazy reaches beyond the Green Line. *Should we give it all up? Compromise on history's gift?* Good one, said the rabbi.

Good one.

V

As I write this, in October 2024, the death toll of Israel's assault on Gaza has surpassed forty thousand, more than two-thirds of these women and children. When I say that I was propagandized at JPPS and Bialik High School, I mean that, having somehow made it outside that bubble, I can no longer talk about Israel or Palestine with my former schoolmates. (The three or four exceptions to this rule are, not coincidentally, among my closest friends today.) It is not about needing agreement: I cannot talk to them for the simple reason that we do not share the same premises. To them, it is a given that the Jewish people have the exclusive right to the Land of Israel (or Judea and Samaria, or the Transjordan, or some other configuration of borders roughly encompassing the same tract of land), for reasons either of their religion or their indigeneity, or both. It is a given that Palestinians hate Jews, that they prefer tyranny to democracy, that they are extremists, and that they self-sabotage when it comes to feeding themselves, educating their children, and building their own infrastructure.* It is a given that the IDF is "the most moral army in the world," that it would never cause harm to civilians unless it were absolutely necessary, and that all of their crimes are in actual fact the crimes of Hamas (or the PLO, or Hezbollah, or Iran, as the case may be), who operate out of civilian infrastructure and use human shields. It is a given that Israel is ready to negotiate; it only lacks a stable partner. It is a given that Israel is a beacon of light within a benighted part of the world. It is a given that a Jew's duty is to

* The "trope of self-sabotage," as Max has put it to me, runs very deep in the decades-long rhetorical strategies of anti-Palestinian commentators and activists. The Palestinians are said to "never miss an opportunity to miss an opportunity" when it comes to getting what they want (e.g., via the Oslo or Camp David processes). Those who parrot this trope, in my experience, can rarely tell you with any degree of accuracy what was offered during negotiations, and which terms were rejected by whom.

support Israel to the hilt. And that which is given is not subject to questioning.

When, in response to the terrorist massacre perpetuated against Israeli civilians by Hamas on October 7, 2023, Israel began indiscriminately bombing Gazans dozens of times a day, promising to cut off electricity and water to a population full of "human animals," in the words of the country's defence minister; when Netanyahu took to television to justify the coming scale and scope of his retaliation by referring to the genocide that God commanded King Saul to perform ("You must remember what Amalek has done to you, says our Holy Bible. And we do remember"); when images of flattened hospitals, schools, homes, grocery stores, playgrounds, restaurants, churches, and mosques began flooding our feeds — I came to appreciate, more starkly than ever, how I had come to traverse two distinct worlds over the short course of my life, worlds that had become two solitudes. Like everyone else in my generation, I receive news and the opinions of others via Instagram, Twitter, and elsewhere. And having grown up with these platforms, I have gathered a motley crew of friends and followers: friends from my school days, from college and grad school and beyond; family both close and distant; strangers. In moments of crisis, the feed evinces a double consciousness that only mirrors my own contradictions. One world cries passionately for an end to the slaughter; the other wipes the blood from its mouth and, in the vocabulary of self-defence, asks for more.

When the so-called war started (the very term implies a certain commensurateness between autonomous nation-states that has no basis in reality), I began sharing information on Twitter and Instagram about the destruction being wrought in Gaza, about murdered journalists (more than 120 as of this writing) and children suffocating beneath the rubble. Some of those close to me asked why I bothered, given that everyone I associated with would already agree with me. I explained that, by an odd twist of circumstance rather than by design, I had a small platform that happened *not* to be inside an echo chamber; there were, in fact, two chambers — and I could choose to speak from one into the other. And lest I appear to be casting myself as courageous, I want to clarify that I did so out of exasperation rather than bravery. I could not believe my eyes when I saw an old classmate repost a video of IDF soldiers playing house in the ruins of a demolished Gazan apartment complex. (This past week, the same person reposted an image of an IDF soldier "reading" a book in a university library to which his company had just set fire.) I wanted to send up what might be the only flare on their horizon that came from someone they could remember as being reasonable, even "one of them." Happily, I reached two or three people, who messaged me privately to say that they were similarly outraged but unwilling to post about it. But generally speaking my tactic failed — the community, such as it was reconstituted on my feed, seemed to close ranks against me almost as soon as I began sharing stories from the other side. I received pushback from all angles. "I'm not going to apologise for Israel defending itself and for the heinous attack on October 7th being the last straw of what we will tolerate from Hamas. We should have decimated that terrorist organisation many years ago," one college classmate wrote to me, adding that "war is messy — you need to have the stomach for it." Someone I only vaguely recall from high school called me an idiot. My own first cousin, once removed, Carol, having heard from someone in the community about my posts, followed me, waited for a day or two until I shared something new, and then began to tell me how all of my information was actually misinformation. Whether it came from the *New York Times*, *B'Tselem*, the BBC, or somewhere else — it was simply false. And my sharing it only exacerbated the antisemitic sentiment being directed at *us*, at our community, at

Jewish people globally. Hadn't I seen the images of the antisemitic signs being hoisted at the pro-Palestine rallies in Montreal and New York? Didn't I realize that pro-Palestinian politics were in fact a cover, a mask for the same old menace? She sent me sixty-eight messages over the course of a few days; I interrupted only to say that I was taking my time to view them.

Eventually I responded to her properly. She has always been kind to me, and I have always liked her. Maybe she represents, for me, the part of the Montreal Jewish community to which I still feel I owe something; the part that raised me, nurtured me, protected me, and — in however biased a manner — educated me; the part that wanted me to succeed and encouraged my ambition; the part that had my back, even when it was turned to them. And maybe I felt that I had seen just enough antisemitism lurking in the comments and on the fringes of anti-Zionist protests to sympathize with her fear, which it would have been wrong to discount as having no justification. What I owed was an explanation, one that attempted to understand her position all while subordinating it to my own. Who knew but that it might get through. So I sent her an email.

An Email from the Author to His First Cousin Once Removed November 15, 2023*

> Dear Carol,
>
> I want to begin this email by saying that I hope that you, A.,† and the children are doing well. It's been far too long since I saw you all. Being out in Paris is wonderful, but I miss my family dearly.

---

* Annotated by the author.

† Her husband. Not his real initial.

It's been a rewarding challenge to begin to look through the materials you've sent me in recent days. Above all, I am approaching them with an open mind and the curiosity I owe you.

In considering how best to respond to you, I've realized that it would be most useful to begin at the beginning, rather than address each of the articles, posts, and reels you very kindly sent my way (the sum of which it'll take me a while to get through!). By "the beginning" I mean your very first question, which is, roughly: what is your position, and why do you hold it?

To address the events of October 7, we need first to condemn them categorically, which I do. But then what? Most pressingly, I think, we need to do what most people with their ears to the ground have been doing for the past month, which is to ask and answer two questions: Why did this happen? and What should be done in response? I think it's notable that the first question asks for a more or less descriptive answer; the second, a more or less prescriptive one.

As to the first, the essential thing to acknowledge is that Hamas's attack was not the product of nothing. It was not the beginning of the events now following in its wake, nor was it the opening salvo of a new war. When the immediate, medium, and long-term histories of the relationship between Israel and Gaza are taken into account, the attacks very quickly emerge in the aspect most appropriate to understanding them — that is, as the latest (if most horrific and appalling) installment in a cycle of violence whose beginning, while debatable, could reasonably be identified as the Nakba/War of Independence. Neither side has been an angel in the history of this conflict, but only one side currently lives under a real, existential threat of annihilation.

When it comes to Gaza, a few facts seem most salient to me: most Gazans now living there never voted for Hamas; the vast majority of Gazans have never left Gaza and are not allowed to leave; what goods enter and leave Gaza is up to Israel, not Gazans; the majority of Gazans know people who were killed by Israeli strikes or bullets despite not being affiliated with Hamas; Benjamin Netanyahu deliberately encouraged the funding and propping-up of Hamas as a strategy to prevent Palestinian political solidarity across the territories. So, here is some context (and much more could be added) for the October 7 attacks that has little to do with a mystifying notion of inherent evil, as some would have it, and much to do with tangible, material, and efficient causes.

The attacks were heinous, unforgivable, and unforgettable. They were savage. And, like all things we call evil, they didn't create themselves. They were caused.

Even if one doesn't agree with the context laid out above, or would quibble with it, the undeniable point is that the attacks came from something — and that "something" is not simply that Hamas hates Jews (although there's also that). It stands to reason that any response that would seek to prevent this kind of thing from happening again would need to understand and address the causes that make up that something, which, in Israel's case, entails taking a long look in the mirror.

So what should be done? I could only begin to answer this myself by trying to find out what feasibly could be done, and then seeing which of the available options seemed most appropriate. Of course, I myself don't know what could really be done. Neither do my friends or brothers or parents or you or the various Israelis and Palestinians we're likely to be acquainted with. We may have a clue, or a sense, or a feeling, but none of us is an expert in diplomacy or military strategy. There are plenty of experts in those areas who are studying the situation and offering possible courses of action. We can read and debate these proposals and see how they fit in with our politics.

What was clear immediately after Israel found, captured, killed, and beat back the terrorists, and after it re-secured the Gazan border and the various checkpoints, was that it did not have to begin levelling apartment blocks, schools, mosques, and hospitals in Gaza. It did not have to cut off gas, water, and electricity to millions. It did not have to instigate the forcible transfer of over a million Palestinians (who now realistically cannot return home). And it did not have to invade Gaza with a ground force. Looking ahead, we can list the things it still does not have to do, including continuing to do all those things and also occupying the territory it promised no longer to occupy over fifteen years ago.

In my opinion, those who argue that Israel does need to do these things in order to prevent another October 7 from happening, or to retrieve the hostages, or to prevent further rocket fire, are making a judgment error. So long as hundreds of thousands of troops are monitoring the Gazan border like hawks (which, notably, they weren't doing under Netanyahu's "safest" government prior to the attacks), no one else is getting through, over, or under those fences. And so long as Israel plans on carpet bombing a region as dense as Gaza and shooting its way through its complex of tunnels, it puts the hostages at a greater, not a lesser, risk, as many have noted. And as for the Hamas rocket attacks, they are still occurring, and they will continue to occur so long as Hamas exists (more on this below), which they will continue to do with or without a ground invasion (anyone who believes that the IDF can actually root out Hamas this way is not listening to the military strategists who have been explaining its impossibility). It stands to reason, then, that if Hamas is going to fire rockets anyway, Israel, at this point in time, has to select between suffering and intercepting rockets and also killing innocent Gazans (and possibly also hostages), or suffering and intercepting rockets without killing innocent Gazans. If the goal is to absolutely end the suffering of Israelis under threat of rocket attack, the approach thus far is proving, and has previously proven, not only ineffective but also wasteful of innocent human life.

It's here that the equation becomes very clear to me. Whatever Hamas decides to do, whatever evil it elects to perpetuate, Israel has the very real option not to respond in kind. We have long ceased to live in a world where the toll exacted for one eye is another eye (let alone ten eyes, which is the current going rate).* What Hamas wants most is what Israel is currently doing to the Palestinians, whom neither government seems to care about. Why should Israel stoop to that? Why should we allow Bibi — a corrupt man surrounded by corrupt and frankly evil advisors — who is out for blood, to convince us that this is the only option? Why let him back our conscience into a corner? Truly supporting Israel would mean doing everything we can to resist this monster of a prime minister and the crimes in which he is trying to make every Jew complicit.

As for the existence of Hamas, it will not depend on Bibi's violent campaign. In fact, they are likely to exist regardless, for a long, long time. There is, unfortunately, an extremist element in every society. This is not an excuse for them. But we know from the history of, say, the War on Terror that placing societies under the pressures of war and bombardment only exacerbates that extremism. The way to root it out is not from the skies, but from the ground — not from the

* As of October 2024, it is over forty-to-one.

authorities above, but from the people below. Those calling for a diplomatic option that prioritizes a ceasefire in the immediate term, hostage negotiations in the medium term (and we know these to be possible, even with Hamas), and the re-development of a democratic, trans-Palestinian statehood politics in the long term, are those to whom we should listen. For their solutions concern the people and their agency as political beings with aspirations like the rest of us. Israel's current policy treats them as a lower form of human than us, and asks us to believe that, as a West Bank settler said to the *New Yorker* in 2023, "my children are prior to the children of the enemy."

I do not accept the argument that civilian casualties simply happen during war, and that therefore the deaths of children, women, and innocent men of Gaza are somehow justified. It is the wrong argument for this situation. It is the argument that Bibi wants us to buy, based on an assumption about this being a "war" he wants us already to have swallowed, and based on an assumption of false necessities, so he can evade responsibility for choosing their deaths over their lives, which could very well have been vouchsafed by way of diplomacy, rather than violent revenge. If he claims that the only solution to the problem of how to respond is to bomb and shoot one's way through, then he is the wrong person to be providing solutions.

While we can argue over sources, over whether this or that bullet really hit this or that person, we cannot argue over the fact that innocent people are dying who should by rights be alive. Innocent people are dying who do not need to die — that is as simply as it can be put, and, to me, as persuasively. Anything Israel pursues in excess of a policy that does everything possible to keep them alive is on its hands, as it is on Hamas's.

Unfortunately, because antisemitism is ubiquitous around the world, what Israel does is increasingly seen as being on our hands as well. I do take and appreciate your point about the seriousness of the uptick in antisemitic attacks and incidents globally in the wake of these events. It is depressing and frightening and we must fight it where we can.

But there are two things to be said on the matter that are routinely ignored. The first has to do with the presence of antisemitism in pro-Palestine marches and protests. This presence is real and ugly. But we should not allow ourselves to be so blinded by it that we believe it to tarnish the Palestinian cause outright. If we are made uncomfortable by how readily some non-Jewish, pro-Palestinian protestors are willing to conflate being Jewish with being a Zionist, we should look in the mirror, for we encourage that conflation ourselves. The conflation was, in fact, the very basis of my education at JPPS and Bialik, where we were taught that to be Jewish was to be a Zionist (why else were we made to recite the Israeli national anthem at school assemblies and events?).

Second, as per your very fair comment about the damage my posting online might do to the

Jewish community we're both a part of, I can only point out that any such damage would be negligible as compared to the tremendous and possibly irreparable reputational damage that the State of Israel has itself done to Jews worldwide since, say, the 1990s. There are many causes of antisemitism, all of them despicable, but it's a sad and regrettable fact that Israel's actions over the past few decades are among them. I know it may be a shocking thing to hear, and the irony is definitely very strong and depressing to me, but I truly cannot think of a single agent more responsible in my lifetime for hatred against Jews living in the West than Israel. It's unfair, because Israel was founded precisely to protect us from antisemites, whose hatred we do not deserve. But in realistic terms, the state is inadvertently turning much of the world against us. Put another way: one can want Israel to do everything it deems necessary for its self-preservation; and one can want antisemitism to decrease worldwide; but unfortunately those two things, as it stands, are in contradiction with one another.

The good news is that the better Israel behaves, the more humanely it treats Palestinians, the more it can do to lessen the amount of antisemitic violence out there — not to say it (or anyone) can ever eliminate antisemitism completely. I don't think it's a coincidence that worldwide antisemitic attacks were at their lowest point during and immediately after the Oslo Accords.

A last, small word on my posting online: if anything, amazingly, I've had the good fortune to have reached some people who didn't previously agree with me. Two or three friends have, because of my voicing an opinion different from that which every Jew in Montreal is asked to adopt, reached out to tell me that they see the situation differently now, and are starting to come around to the shades of grey that exist between Netanyahu and Hamas. From the limited and anecdotal evidence I have, then, my posting has only done a modest amount of good.

It was not an easy feeling to realize, near the end of high school, that I had spent the whole of my young life hearing one kind of message. It has taken me a long time to hear the others, and to piece together something like a narrative that takes all of them into account. At least, that's what I try to do. When I post, specifically to the small audience I have, I am trying to get people to listen to some of these other voices.

You, Carol, are my family and my elder. I will always love my family and respect my elders, and I hope I haven't failed on either of those fronts, in your eyes, as you've read this email. I have only tried, here, to sketch out why I hold the position I hold.

Sincerely,
Ben

VI

On a recent trip to Montreal with my partner, a month before the "war," I agreed to show her the outside of Bialik High School. (The building now houses both Bialik and JPPS — the latter was moved from the building I went to for seven years due to declining attendance rates at both schools.) She wanted to see with her own eyes the site of the many incredible (one would be forgiven for saying *tall*) tales I had told her, about invented sports and phobic physics teachers and much else. We were staying at my parents' house, and I knew the way by heart. The drive took about twenty minutes. It had once bothered me that I didn't live where my friends lived: I was only one of two of my peers who didn't live in Hampstead or Côte Saint-Luc, the island's largest Jewish enclaves, or Westmount, where the wealthiest among us lived. At some point, I became proud of the fact that we were different, that my parents had elected to live in a suburb with more different kinds of people (even if all of us belonged to the same middle-upper-middle class bracket).

The school sits on a cul-de-sac, where the road loops to allow drivers to turn back around. I noticed that the soccer field, which used to be uneven and poorly mown, had been replaced with a new one. The track ringing the perimeter was a bright terracotta. Otherwise, the building looked exactly the same. I always thought it had the shape of an insect, with two broad, orthogonal legs stretching out on either side. Facing the school from the other side of the loop is a Chabad house. I remember watching it get built, week by week, from the classroom where I took Tanakh class in ninth grade.* One day, there was a mound of dirt about three storeys high; in the winter we discussed the possibility of sledding down it. A year later, an entire building stood in its place. In my last two years of high school, the day would end with us spilling out of school, desperate to get home or to our friends' houses, only to be confronted by members of the Chabad asking us if we wanted to

* This class involved the mostly secular study of the Hebrew Bible.

put on tefillin or shake the *lulav*,* or perform some other religious function. This seemed a significant moment in the evolution of Bialik from a secular, folkish, socialist, and Zionist institution to the confused muddle of ethno-religious ideas it had become by the time I attended.

Idling in the car between those two buildings, I entertained the idea that Bialik was not to blame for its internal contradictions, nor for the myopic world view it imparted to its students. The school today is the symptom of our broken self-conception as North American Jews. What they couldn't tell us in class, for not quite knowing it themselves, was that Jewish history had stopped in 1948. This, anyway, was the logical outcome of adopting their perspective. For to join the past like all things that are and were, to be borne down the river along with everything else we wish, in ways both noble and horrid, to remember, is to become historicizable — to be made relative to what came before and to what is yet to come, to become what *was*, with all its anomalies, and so to shuffle off the illusion of infallibility. If history is the manner in which we narrativize the past, and if we refuse to allow our postwar experience to be narrated *as* past, then we refuse to become a part of history as such. This is one way to explain the enormous social backlash faced by the Israeli New Historians who, in the 1980s, studied newly unclassified documents pertaining to the founding of the State of Israel in order to write the history of the Nakba. Holocaust is perpetually yesterday and tomorrow, and Israel is perpetually the present. An eternal present that cannot become a question, cannot grow old, cannot fade, cannot become a mistake, and cannot be reconciled with any history I know of. It cannot *become*. And so long as our Jewry is tied to its exhausted reasons and its stubborn

* The *lulav* is a bundle of three plants and a citrus fruit (known as the four species) — palm frond (*lulav*), myrtle (*hadass*), willow (*aravah*), and citron (*etrog*) — used during the Jewish autumn holiday of Sukkot.

insistence on its *now*, we will continue to believe and assert things about ourselves that are true only within the world view that we alone uphold, while the rest of the planet rolls on. We will continue to see ourselves as fresh victims, incapable of inflicting harm upon others (let alone committing genocide); we will continue to think about our politics in terms belonging to the previous century; and we will continue to be blind to the world and the people in it. Bialik and the March are two of our many cherished time capsules, in which old ideologies inadequate to our times lie mummified. You, the reader, may know of yet others. Try as we might to reanimate them, as a crank of the wheel reanimates the automaton, they have no valid life of their own. As the rest of the world creates the actual present by daily consigning and writing itself into history, we risk remaining stuck in place.

But not all of us. I'd like to imagine that Dov Ber Borochov, were he alive today, would ally himself with those leftist Jews around the world who reject all such ahistorical thinking. If his commitment to dialectical materialism were true, he would surely have come to see that the Jewish people could not be forcibly proletarianized — indeed that there would be no point to this — that the Jewish socialist cause should be joined to the international socialist cause (after his death in 1917, his followers did indeed bring his spirit into the Communist Party of the Soviet Union), and therefore that no nationalist political solution would be needed for the Jewish people. And even if we concede the necessity of providing a homeland to the Jewish people after the trauma of the Holocaust — the need to intervene *then* — there are those of us today who understand that solidarity with the oppressed is the more pressing Jewish question for the twenty-first century than Zionism. The friends and heroes of mine who march as Jews for Palestine in Montreal, New York, and Paris, who confront censorship in German periodicals and swinging batons on Berlin's Sonnenallee, and who advocate for Gazans down the boulevards of Tel Aviv — it is they who carry the torch for a Jewry that has long felt responsible for *tikkun olam*, for the universe that is saved each time one life is saved, and for resisting the temptation to tribalize.

But the good has not yet defeated the bad. More people die each hour — an additional twelve thousand Palestinians have been killed since I began writing this section of the present chapter. From the Instagram accounts of people I used to see at parties, people I used to like or love or desire, commune with and listen to, I read that it is antisemitic to suggest that Israelis are capable of genocide. *Time Magazine* and the *Atlantic* said so. I read that Bibi had no other choice. I read that we have to defend what is ours, that they are trying to take it all away from us.

As we drove home, the streets of Côte Saint-Luc and Hampstead were sunny and calm and quiet. They remain that way. People lay down their heads; they sleep easy. Dogs chase each other through the park while the crack of a baseball leaving a bat sounds off nearby. Time, and what to do with it, and how to seize it, is ignored. Its passage is registered only in the lines on people's faces. The rabbi at Bialik once joked that the urban planner for the Garden of Eden had spent his school years looking over the shoulder of the urban planner for Côte Saint-Luc. We were on the top floor of the school and could see the train tracks running along the other side of the soccer field. *And what now?* I could have asked. *Should we give it all up?*

Good one.

Chapter 4

Wish I Could Go Back

All this resting-place Earth   shall become empty

—"The Wanderer"

In the autumn of 2018, when I first began in earnest to sift through the documents I had acquired in Vienna, I was often on the verge of tears. It was not simply the tragedy of the Sternschusses' displacement, of the loved ones never to be seen again, of abstracted trauma made palpable again. It was stranger than that. They were bittersweet tears.

I would turn over a photo of Max, Anna's brother. A headshot, taken at any old photography studio for use in a passport or some other official documentation. But the occasion of the photograph — the still air in the studio, the smell of the white tarp pulled down for a backdrop, the slight constriction of the lapels against the chest, crimping the necktie, the stress, perhaps, of needing this document *now,* of being under the bureaucratic thumb, of feeling one's collar grow ever tighter with each passing day, of realizing history is happening to one, now — came flooding back to me. Flooding *back.*

An absurdity, but not an anomaly. This moment had nothing to do with me, properly speaking. And intellectually I not only knew but counted on this fact. How to approach the past without forcing it into a ready-made structure — this was my aim. And yet my attempt at sketching a history was being invaded by *going back*; that is, by nostalgia. I longed to return to that moment, to Max. But I had him there, in my hand, in a rectangle

of photographic paper nearly one hundred years old, as much and as close I had ever had him, or ever will. Return where? Return how?

In those moments I had to put everything aside. Collapse the spread of papers into a pile and slip the photographs back among them. See the dark grain of my desktop again. Was such a history possible? In *The Unbearable Lightness of Being*, Kundera's narrator, expressing what it means in truth to live without the eternal recurrence of events, writes that "everything is illuminated by the aura of nostalgia, even the guillotine." He admits to feeling nostalgic while perusing old portraits of Hitler, at whose hands several of his family members perished, because the images returned him to his childhood. He was peering into the "profound moral perversity of a world that rests essentially on the nonexistence of return, for in this world everything is pardoned in advance and therefore everything cynically permitted." But it is in this world that we live and breathe; and it is here that we ask the past to speak to us, here that we read what is called time by writing what is called history upon the traces of its passage. Kundera forgot to add that in this world, in addition to everything being permitted, nothing is understood. We see the crimp in an old tie, long ago obliterated, and weep for not having fixed it.

I

Every August, at the end of summer camp, we used to sing the same song. It was a version of "Stay" meant to convey the simple fact that none of us wanted to return home to our parents and the start of a new school year. "Why can't we stay at camp / just a little bit longer?"

And we felt that old feeling. Is there a more common or universal one? Having come to the end of something, we long to be back at the beginning again. Or maybe: having learned, through time, to appreciate something we have been experiencing, we long to go back and plant that appreciation from the very beginning. But the laws of nature cannot be contravened. Next time, we promise, we'll live in the moment. We'll live in it so fully that we won't even be capable of nostalgia, when the moment's gone.

But what is it, really? We know it when we feel it. And yet there is some serious confusion about its basic meaning. We return down the well-trod path of its etymology: *nostos algos*, "homecoming sorrow." It sounds ancient but was coined in the 1680s by an Alsatian-Swiss medical student at the University of Basel to describe something felt by soldiers who had ventured far away from their homelands. He was naming a medical condition, to be precise. It seems significant that the pain experienced was not for home itself, but for the act of returning home — the ritual of going back, perhaps a little changed, perhaps a lot, to the place where one began. Homecoming, though, is not just about going back: it's about being *received*, being welcomed, by the people who stayed behind and the place that didn't change at all (or if it did, then much less in comparison). If everyone and everything changed in equal proportion, there would be no pain. Or it would be very different.

This is not where the confusion lies. Johannes Hofer, the student who named this malady we all seem to be afflicted with, must have been talking about a spatial relation. "Nostalgia describes the melancholy that originates from the desire to return to one's homeland," he wrote in reference to the Swiss mercenaries who had been sent to Gaul. The return would have been quite literal — a prolonged displacement from point B back to point A. The soldier straps his boots and marches on to lands unknown. There, hungry, sleep-deprived, gangrenous, surrounded by rough strangers and far away from the place where he was raised, he yearns to go back. "How often have I lain beneath rain on a strange roof, thinking of home," Darl says in *As I Lay Dying.* That could have been anybody from any time in the human epoch. It could well have been the "lord" in the "Wife's Lament," an Old English poem that is at least a thousand years old. The titular wife, thinking mournfully on her husband who "departed from his people / over tossing waves," imagines his nostalgia for their shared homeland. Here is a modern English translation:

> I believe my lord sits
> by a stony storm-beaten cliff,
> that water-tossed my weary friend
> sits in a desolate home. He must suffer
> much in his mind, remembering too often
> a happier place. Woe unto him
> who languishing waits for a loved one.

Home is a place, and one's distance from it is measured in many sad miles.

But what about all that time? Only a moment ago I was saying that nostalgia was a matter of beginnings and endings, of time-wrought change, the Vienna of 1938 and that of 2024, not of *here* and *there*. Actually, spatial separation on its own can do little to make us nostalgic: waiting in line at the grocery store across town, I may want more than anything to be home; but I am not nostalgic for home. Time would seem to be required. We hardly need to be told that nostalgia is a function of memory, and therefore of the passage of time. Shakespeare gives us the finest expression of this point in Sonnet 30:

> When to the sessions of sweet silent thought
> I summon up remembrance of things past,
> I sigh the lack of many a thing I sought,
> And with old woes new wail my dear time's waste:

From the vantage of the present, we conjure the past and feel, excruciatingly, the gulf between them. We pile new wail onto old woe in the process — this is the *algos*. For good reason, C.K. Scott Montcrieff reached back for Shakespeare when giving a title to his translation of Proust's *À la recherche du temps perdu*. That novel is both the study and performance of nostalgia as a temporally mediated phenomenon. The moments of "involuntary memory" that punctuate the narrative — the fragrant madeleine, the wobbly cobblestone — all produce in the narrator the lack of many a thing he once sought (or felt, or did). But equally and on top of this, the novel upholsters its own narrative with an additional layer of nostalgia when, in the last volume, we come to understand that the tale we have been reading is the product of its own final moments, when the narrator discovers his vocation as a novelist. The reader becomes nostalgic for a time before he knew this information — for the early moments on the subway or in cafés or in the dim intervals before sleep when he was first brought into this fictive world of which he is now a veteran. "Three years, many pauses, copies lost on planes, Liverpool, Stockholm, New York, Berlin, Philadelphia, Edinburgh, Paris (where I saw his bed)," the critic David Hering wrote of finishing Proust's masterwork. "You don't read it, you live it." You live the sorrow of time lost, and the effort to find it again.

Is the home to which we return a place, then? Or a time? You'd be tempted to say both. But really, "home" is a red herring. *Nostos* is a mistake in the coinage. It was only accurate in the sense that Hofer needed a Greek term for an existing German term, *Heimweh*, in order to legitimize it as a medical concept within the academy. As Hofer knew, the francophone Swiss mercenaries already had a term for *Heimweh* in their own language: *mal du pays*. People still say this. (It was at that time so peculiar to the Swiss, in fact, that it was sometimes mockingly referred to as *le mal du Suisse* or *Schweizerheimweh*, in German.) And in English, of course, we have our own rendering. "Homesickness," which the English speaker knows to be different from nostalgia, is what Hofer was really getting at: the desire to be back where one is safe and comfortable.* In summer camp, tossing and turning on my lumpy cot, I was often homesick for my house back in Montreal; but I was never nostalgic for it.

There is no need to litigate whether home is a place in space or in time. Nostalgia has little to do with it; any connections are incidental. What matters in "homecoming" is the latter term — the notion of return, or recurrence. A thing must happen, or must be imagined to happen, twice. But time must intervene: there can be no nostalgia in simultaneity, which is the domain of doppelgängers (*how can he be me while I am me?*) and déjà-vu (*how can this already have happened while it is currently happening?*). The intervention of time is important, because time produces the impasse that gives this common feeling its potency. Nostalgia indexes something we already know, namely that nothing really happens twice. *First as tragedy then as farce.* Is there a more nostalgic line in all of Western thought? Remembering, going back, retreading the same ground: each of these is a farce in the generic sense of the term — ridiculous, absurd, extravagant, improbable, nonsensical. Time's arrow only points one way, famously. And the entropy it produces cannot be reversed. Nostalgia is a defence mechanism against the ruthlessness of time's passage.

Nostalgia is thus always tragic, fuelled by the irony attending a great effort that was futile to begin with. You are always, in one way or another, returning to loss. The childhood whose traces you seek

---

* This corrective also makes sense of nostalgia being once seen as a malady. Homesickness is often something we think to correct in children (at camp or boarding school, for example); one ought to learn, so our pedagogy goes, to be physically removed from one's retreat and place of comfort. Seen this way, as homesickness, Hofer's version of *le mal du pays* becomes suddenly continuous with our own: a childish or primitive feeling we try to subdue in various domains of human life. The other nostalgia — that is, the feeling we commonly know by that name today — is something else. We tend not to correct it but rather to nurture it. It is not an aberration but an affect.

upon homecoming is gone. "That old feeling" can only be accessed as an insinuation, now. Odysseus may regain his queen and his kingdom, but he has lost ten years to wandering, and another ten to war. "That is the land of lost content, / I see it shining plain," A.E. Housman wrote. "The happy highways where I went / And cannot come again." The tragedy of nostalgia gains its texture by the fact that it entails the loss not only of time but also innocence. "Every act of rebellion expresses a nostalgia for innocence and an appeal to the essence of being," Camus wrote. I never did figure out what the essence of being was, but I know what he meant about rebellion. Being in the world brings forth knowledge, and knowledge is a curse, a certain kind of mental entropy. Sooner or later, one's hand is forced, one knows too much, a break must be made. *Why did you force my hand?* This is the rebel's question to the world; things were better before I knew just how bad they could be. Within the first act of rebellion the first moment of nostalgia was already seeded: the temptation represented by the tree of knowledge was not its existence, but the *knowledge* of its existence; it was the *knowing* that foredoomed the first man and woman to eat of the tree's fruit and to wish, while chewing, that they had never been made aware of its presence in the first place.

Nostalgia partakes of the same sort of desire that prompts us to rake the air for the words that ought not to have left our mouths but did. Can it all be put back into the bottle? It is a common human reflex, a spasm of exasperation, in the face of an impossibility. We like to use the metaphor of Pandora's box to make sense of world-historical events and their irrevocable consequences. But it is not so rare an occurrence as that. The box is being opened all the time, day by day, minute by minute, as we lie awake at night beneath roofs once foreign to us, wishing we could go back, when or where it doesn't quite matter, waiting with that sinking feeling in our stomachs as the sand runs and runs and runs through our fingers.

II

In our time, nostalgia is mostly something that has been manufactured for mass consumption. One should be skeptical of it as a rule.

The other month, I went to the gigantic cinema complex at Les Halles to watch *The Holdovers*, a coming-of-age drama about a classics teacher at a New England prep school who is tasked with looking after the handful of students who, for one reason or another, have nowhere to go during winter break. "The movie isn't feel-good," the critic A.S. Hamrah writes. "Set in 1970, it is nostalgic." But nostalgic for whom? Sitting beside a Southeast Asian and a European, I was the only one of us who had any real-life connection with the place being depicted. I had spent many winters in and around New England; I knew the strange sensation of standing outside with frozen toes on a darkened afternoon coloured by Christmas lights, feeling nevertheless that the blankets of snow covering the roofs and lawns made everything wonderfully bright. But the effect was not reserved for me alone. In fact, whatever "true" referents my nostalgia pointed to were equally balanced by many false ones. The movie is set in the 1970s. And when Paul Giamatti's wall-eyed, curmudgeonly prep school teacher takes his two companions, a school cook grieving for her lost son and a student from a broken home, to Boston, I felt overcome with that well-worn sorrow, a longing to return not simply to Boston, but to Boston in 1970, a location in space-time I had never been to. (I thought, in fact, of my father, who *had* been in Boston in the 1970s, and whose potential feelings of nostalgia I was now, somehow, accessing for myself in the conditional tense.)

"We are homesick most for the places we have never known," in Carson McCullers's famous formulation. Replace "homsesick" with "nostalgic" this time and the underlying idea is undeniable. This is a troubling thought: we can long to return to places and times we've never been to. The very notion of *return* is vitiated, and yet this doesn't seem to matter. People can and do exploit this fact. (*Why do I feel like I've been here before? Have we met somewhere? I feel like I knew you in another life.* These are among the clichés that account for the return that is not a return.) Much of the art of our present, the so-called postmodern age, is built upon nostalgia for periods and places that have little to do with the person consuming the art. In his book *Generation X*, the novelist Douglas Coupland famously called this cultural tendency "legislated nostalgia," defining it as if it were a verb: "To force a body of people to have memories they do not actually possess."

They may also have little to do with those actual periods and places themselves. Fredric Jameson, the eminent theorist of postmodernism, pointed out that cultural representations of the 1950s produced after (or at the end of) the 1950s themselves "evoke" the era not by unearthing its "historical realities," but by mobilizing a list of "stereotypes, of *ideas* of facts and historical realities."* They are many: "Main Street, U.S.A.; Marilyn Monroe; a world of neighbours and PTAs; small retail chain stores," etc. Whatever was true of the 1950s, there exists, as if in parallel, the compendium of things that make up the 1950s as we "know" them. In the culture industry, nostalgia trades in images and not facts, in the signs of eras and their realities, which have been imprinted upon us as genuinely as our own experiences. We feel them with equal pathos. The same applies in politics. "Make America Great Again," for example: the late-night talk-show hosts love nothing more than to send their comedian correspondents into the heartland to ask their unsuspecting dupes when, exactly, America was last great. Before desegregation? Before women had the vote? Before emancipation? Some are bold enough to admit their racism and their

* Emphasis mine.

sexism on camera. But most stutter and squirm in the grips of the trap. The exercise gets a laugh from the self-satisfied among us, but it also misses the point. The slogan points to no actual referent in the world, but to an idea, a floating fantasy unmoored from any particular time and place. In the past, America was always great, because in the past things were always better and more innocent. As a form of emotional currency, nostalgia turns out to be very cheap. For an artist or for a politician, my enthusiasm and my indignation come at pretty penny. But my longing for the good old days?

We're on the brink, now, of admitting that there are two sorts of nostalgia: the kind that ties us to our "lived experiences," and the kind that ties us to familiar illusions. Then again, what do we really mean by the first? We treat the past like a foreign country, to paraphrase L.P. Hartley's famous saying — it may require some effort, but we can travel there and traverse its terrain. But is there really a past as such, outside of our representation of it in memory? And if not, then what does it mean to go there, as if there's truly a *there* there? I recall my childhood. I recall sitting on a stone bench at the top of Mount Washington, my bowl cut tossed across my forehead by the wind. I recall huddling into the soft cotton of a hand-me-down teal sweatshirt (my hands disappear above the cuffs). I recall hugging my knees and smiling, seated beside my two older brothers. Am I now returning to this moment? Or am I returning to the framed photograph of it that sits on a shelf in my parents' living room?

Maybe there is only one type of nostalgia. Maybe we are always yearning to go back to the idea of a thing, and not to the thing itself, even when speaking of our own childhoods. Maybe it's futile to adjudicate whether one longs to return to somewhere one knows, or somewhere one never could have been in the first place — for the simple reason that such a place or time never really existed. Or not in that way.

Maybe it's all one currency. We keep pushing the coin in the slot to make time speak of itself in tenses. We hope the game will play itself differently, for once, but it can't. "Where did the steed go? Where the young warrior?" the wanderer in another Old English poem laments. "How the time has passed / gone under night helm / as if it never was." As if.

Was life really perfect, or better, or purer in the Garden? It doesn't really matter. All we have is the image, and the image is all.

III

Nostalgia's fixation on the past should not overshadow nostalgia's dominion in the future. What we mean when we say that time's arrow only points one way, and that nostalgia is our reaction to this fact, is that we are raging against the future into which we are perpetually being pushed. Like Walter Benjamin's Angel of History, we have turned our faces away from it, even as time propels us in its direction. A disproportionate focus on the time that slips away from us into the past neglects the simple fact that motion is relative: we are equally pulling away from the present into the future.

"You can suffer nostalgia in the presence of the beloved if you glimpse a future where the beloved is no more," Kundera wrote. Nostalgia's most potent use of the future tense lies in this common, heart-rending exercise. The future is where our present becomes past; if we can project ourselves there, we will long to return to the moment we are currently in and feel sorrow about its imminent passage into what was. You could argue that every experience of nostalgia is doubled in this way: the painful awareness that one cannot truly return to *there* and *then* already contains the awareness that one will not be able to return to *here* and *now*. Nothing could be more natural than to imagine our present as past, given that life is the perpetual witnessing of this very transformation.

This means that our present, too, is something we never experience as such, but only ever as a sign of itself. W.G. Sebald understood this better than most. Take the peregrinations of his narratological stand-in through Suffolk County, England, in *The Rings of Saturn*. The county, which through its long history enjoyed two or three separately prosperous periods as a fishery hub, a country getaway for industrialists, a weapons research site, etc., is by the end of the twentieth century a sort of graveyard. The coastline and the inland landscapes are dotted by all manner of rubble and ruin — medieval towers, crumbling manors, rusted railways — but also much else that is nondescript and hard to place without a keen historical eye. The real thrust of the novel is not so much the travel itself as it is the narrator's nostalgic encounter with these ruins. Whether he stumbles upon an old tombstone or the conspicuous emptiness of a centuries-old town, Sebald experiences these features of the landscape as an historical access. The path he follows is nostalgic by nature, consisting of a cascading series of digressions that collectively breathe the past of Suffolk County into the silent slumber of its present decay. This inflation is a kind of artificial life that illuminates the sediments of time layered within an otherwise unmoving place.

Like his intellectual forebears of the Romantic era, Sebald understood the ruin and the wreck to provide the perfect condensation of nostalgia's parasitic relationship with time. In a way we project ourselves onto the old stones, urging them to speak woefully of the time before their dilapidation, and of the second melancholy to come, when we ourselves shall be as little evident on the earth as the great societies that once knew this rubble as part of an edifice. Like Scipio Africanus gazing upon the inferno consuming Carthage, we are called to weep before ruined things, not only for all that has been lost to time, but also all that will soon join it.

Or, if it's a bit uncouth to weep like that, we can brood, as Sebald does while roaming the halls of Somerleyton Hall in Suffolk.

Alas, the manor is no longer what it was. As he wanders through the dilapidation of Somerleyton, which once struck the visitor "as an oriental palace in a fairy tale," Sebald notes that "the glass-covered walks and the palm house, whose lofty dome used once to light up the nights, were burnt out in 1913 after a gas explosion and subsequently demolished." He adds: "[One cannot] readily say which decade or century it is, for many ages are superimposed here and coexist." What's telling here is that, though the hall could not be more different now from its years of grandeur, still, for Sebald, those years are sedimented within it irrevocably, such that even in its decrepit state Somerleyton bears within it its own historicity, the way each of us carries the past within us in the form of traces, ideas, and mementos.

The story of Somerleyton is the story of the entire region of Suffolk, for Sebald. It is a tale of a part of the country that has played host to the vampiric needs of proto-capitalism and industrial capitalism. It experienced the wild swings of boom and bust, as industrialists built their grand country homes there, only to sell them and leave them in destitution once they'd gone bankrupt twenty years later. It is a land scarred by the whipping winds of contingency, and it thus has little organic development that has outstripped the vulture-like grip of economic forces emanating from London. It is time's open wound made manifest on earth, a site for the spectacle of nostalgia on a social, rather than individual, scale. To encounter Suffolk in the present is to return to it via a shimmering montage of all that it ever was, and all that it never shall be.

The hint of negativity about the future, here, is no accident. It is the product of the end-of-history mentality out of which the novel struggles to emerge. If we were to rewrite *The Rings of Saturn* as a Romantic-era travelogue, we might look at its curious ruins as merely the necessary civilizational decay that begets rebirth on history's path to progress. In the Hegelian mindset common to that earlier period, ruination gives rise, in dialectical fashion, to something better and more enlightened. But not for Sebald — and not for us. Call it our congenital defect, or capitalist realism, but we long ago ceased to envision any alternatives to our present condition. We believe in the dialectic of history the way most Americans believe in God; that is, rhetorically. In temperament, and in our most nostalgic moods, each of us is an Angel of History, who sees "one single catastrophe which keeps piling wreckage upon wreckage and hurls it in front of his feet. The angel would like to stay, awaken the dead and make whole what has been smashed." But "a storm is blowing from Paradise; it has got caught in his wings with such violence that the angel can no longer close them."

◈ ◈ ◈

In the seventeenth century, nostalgia was something to be cured — for example, with opium, leeches, and a trip to the mountains. Now it is a basic ingredient of most films, pop songs, bestsellers, and the starter packs and moody montages that float around social media. Nostalgia theorists and scholars would probably object to the ahistorical view of nostalgia sketched above. Thomas Mallon, for example, explains that in the nineteenth century it "was regarded as more a geographic longing than a temporal one," emphasizing its protean nature. Svetlana Boym sees it as a social phenomenon that can swell into an epidemic or recede into an ambient mood. "The twentieth century began with a futuristic utopia and ended with nostalgia," she writes.

But Mallon also wonders "if [nostalgia] isn't a neurological condition, something fundamental and immune to the vagaries of history." Maybe it is a part of us no matter what. *Mais où sont les neiges d'antan?* I can't but feel that François Villon is with me now as he was with readers of his century. He proves a feeling for all time, immortalized in poetry.

And maybe it had to be poetry. It is said that we invented verse as a device for memory-keeping. When Homer sang to his assemblies, before the written word, he was opening the valve to a vast cultural repository. The people listened and smiled; they raged and they wept. They remembered with him. But what they remembered hadn't happened to them, if it had happened at all. His song, like so many that have followed it, delivered the fantasy of return to a phantasmic point in space and time. Imagining Odysseus straining against all to return — to his home, to those he had left behind, to the state of innocence that had been swept up in the tides of war and taken from him — they were imagining themselves. All our literature of memory, whether individual or cultural or national, is a technology against time, suffused with the tragedy of a futile optimism; nostalgic.

> The days gone by
> Come back upon me from the dawn almost
> Of life; the hiding-places of my power
> Seem open, I approach, and then they close;
> I see by glimpses now, when age comes on
> May scarcely see at all; and I would give
> While yet we may, as far as words can give,
> A substance and a life to what I feel:
> I would enshrine the spirit of the past
> For future restoration.

These lines from *The Prelude*, which Wordsworth wrote at the behest of his friend Samuel Taylor Coleridge and rewrote several times over the course of his life, reflect the poet's attempt to grapple with the French Revolution, whose emergence and failure simultaneously ended the *ancien régime* and foreclosed a radically democratic future only briefly glimpsed. The poet was mourning a past whose potential was never, in his lifetime, fulfilled. Whoever would enshrine the spirit of the past finds that he can only enshrine its image. But that has never dampened the verve, has never quelled the storm blowing from Paradise. And it has always been enough. Every August, at the end of summer camp, we used to sing the same song. Having come to the end of something. Having come to the end. Our libraries are full of so many reckless attempts to stand in the same river twice.

Chapter 5

The Third Solitude

Love consists in this, that two solitudes protect, and touch, and greet each other.

— **Rainer Maria Rilke**

In Montreal the dominant ethnic groups stare at one another balefully across their self-erected ghetto walls. Three solitudes.

— **Irving Layton**

Grandpa, how could you so quickly cease being French, and what a pity for me.

— **Marie Uguay**

We who belong to this city have never left The Church.

— **Leonard Cohen, "Montreal"**

I

When I was eleven years old, I learned in school that the first colonist in Canada died a very Canadian death. Louis Hébert had been born in Paris, in 1575, to an apothecary and his well-to-do wife. Though Louis's father, Nicolas Hébert, was a typical bourgeois, his mother, Jacqueline, had been married before to an aristocrat; by grace of the law, her new husband Nicolas inherited both the assets and the filial responsibilities of her well-off previous husband. Thus, despite his father being a member of the professional class (which at the time would have been lumped under the third estate), Louis was brought up in some of the grandest residences in Paris, and watched a couple of his half-siblings take oaths and enter the clergy. Louis himself was not destined for the cloth, preferring instead to follow in his father's footsteps and learn the secrets of pharmacology.

Forty years before Louis's birth, in 1534, news first reached France that Jacques Cartier had found and claimed territory in the New World for King Francis I. He had been searching for a passage to Asia and spared no effort to attain his goal.* The men on the expedition slaughtered nearly one thousand great auks for food on Îles aux Oiseaux. From either the Mi'kmaq or the Haudenosaunee (whom the French and generations of Canadians insisted on calling the Iroquois), whose members he encountered in Chaleur Bay and Gaspé Bay, respectively, Cartier learned that the leaves of an evergreen known as aneda (or anneda) could stave off scurvy; he consequently supplied it to his men.† Before pointing his ships back toward France, Cartier seemed to have thought that planting a

* Upon his return to France, Cartier maintained that the land he had just visited was a part of Asia.

† To this day, it remains unclear precisely which plant "aneda" was. It was most likely *Abies balsamea*, or possibly *Thuja occidentalis*.

ten-metre cross bearing the phrase "Vive le Roi de France" on the great thumb of the Gaspé Peninsula would make his territorial claim a matter of fact. He might not have guessed that it would take the better part of a century to establish a lasting colony there. As the expedition set off, certain of returning soon enough once the king learned of his success, Cartier kidnapped two men who were sons to Donnacona, chief of the St. Lawrence Haudenosaunee village of Stadacona. He brought them to France as living artifacts from his voyage and returned with them to Canada on his second expedition, the following year. This time around, while preparing to return to Saint-Malo once more, Cartier kidnapped Donnacona himself; he wanted the venerable chief to repeat to the royal court what he had told Cartier and his men — that there was kingdom called Saguenay, rich in gold, rubies, and much else, on an island somewhere north of the St. Lawrence River. It is said that Donnacona received a warm and hospitable welcome in France. But what he likely wanted most was for Cartier to return him — and the eight of his Haudenosaunee kinsmen who had been similarly displayed before astonished French eyes — to Stadacona "within twelve moons," as promised. Thirty-six moons passed before Donnacona died in Paris, never to see his home again. For his part, Cartier got what he had wanted out of the old chief: more ships, funding for a third voyage west, and a mandate to discover the great (and ultimately mythical) Kingdom of Saguenay and plunder its riches for France.

The 1530s were, therefore, optimistic times for the kingdom. But the mood would quickly sour: the Wars of Religion, which would see the deaths of roughly three million people, exploded in 1562, forcing France's gaze from the wider world back to its domestic territories and the enemies along its borders. The Héberts themselves, despite being protected by wealth and privilege, would not have been immune to the tensions coursing through Paris. In fact, had a curious, fifteen-year-old Louis decided to take a summer stroll in 1590 and climb the northern ramparts of the city walls that then encircled the capital, he would have witnessed a distant black assembly of twenty-five thousand Protestant troops, commanded by King Henry IV of France (who had not yet converted to Catholicism)* swarming the slopes of Montmartre. In the distance, the smouldering remains of windmills, to which Henry had set fire, might have seemed to Louis like so many wrecked castles from the fantastical tales and fables of his childhood. The king's men regularly bombarded Paris from their vantage on the hill but lacked the artillery to take the city by force. A siege would have to do. And though it would ultimately fail in the face of a Spanish-Catholic axis, in the four months before Henry ordered the siege broken and his troops to fall back, nearly fifty thousand Parisians would die of starvation. Louis, who would have experienced hunger and soaring food prices, might well have seen these starved men, women, and children littering the streets and gutters of Paris. They comprised, after all, more than one-fifth of the city's 230,000 residents.

We wouldn't want to overdetermine Louis's decision to study the healing properties of plants and potions. It was the family business, and it went back a long way with them. But Louis knew death, desperation, and the fervent, often fatal, passions of religious conviction from a young age. One can't help but see something calmly defiant in the decision to study the cultivation and use of those elements that would give and prolong life. Between 1595 and 1600, during which time Henry put a partial end to the conflict between the Catholics and the Huguenots, Louis discovered the various uses and properties of the plants, fruits, and roots that comprised the pharmacological canon of his time. In himself, he discovered a diligent and attentive student with a

* In a bid to have Paris, a resolutely Catholic and anti-Huguenot city, capitulate to his rule, Henry would convert to Catholicism in 1593, reportedly proclaiming that "Paris is well worth a mass."

remarkably green thumb. At the end of his studies, Louis set up shop as a licensed apothecary, confirming himself as a member of the bourgeoisie. He reinforced his respectability in 1601 with a sensible marriage to Marie Rollet, a young, resourceful girl from a good family, as the biographers attest.

Perhaps the turbulence of his earlier years was responsible for Louis's inability to sit still. Despite having set up a successful business and having purchased a modest home on the banks of the Seine for his fledgling family, in 1606 he found himself inking a deal with Pierre Dugua, explorer and recently appointed lieutenant general of New France, to provide his apothecarial services for one year to the small outpost of Frenchmen then exploiting the natural resources of eastern Canada. The appeal of New France was likely not sudden for him: his cousin Claude had married the Baron de Poutrincourt, who had been to New France under Dugua's command, in 1604, to found a colony at Saint-Croix on the Bay of Fundy with seventy-nine settlers. Thirty-five of these men died of scurvy — "land sickness," as they called it — marking a disastrous and dispiriting turn in the French colonization effort. But Samuel de Champlain, who would shortly found the city of Quebec (the first permanent European settlement in New France), had also been on the 1604 expedition. Being a skilled cartographer, his reconnaissance of the coastline, which could not have been undertaken without the assistance of Passamaquoddy guides, led him to see that a settlement on the northern shores of what is now Nova Scotia would be easier to maintain. This outpost, which the French called Port-Royal, was granted by Dugua to Louis's cousin-in-law, Poutrincourt; and it was here that Louis had been commissioned to go and ply his trade.

He arrived there without difficulty. And in no time at all Louis had risen to the top of the pioneers' estimation. (Admittedly, given the gruelling conditions on that windswept bit of Canadian coastline, the competition was not likely to have been stiff.) He took to his work with great zeal, learning from the Mi'kmaq which indigenous herbs and roots were useful for which ailments. He experimented with land cultivation and plant propagation, developing what could be called a sustainable and local agricultural setup for his practice. He was consequently able to treat and cure the hardy soldiers, traders, and fur-trappers who populated the settlement and who were grateful to have such a knowledgeable and good-humoured healer within their midst. They were no doubt distressed to see Louis leave Port-Royal at the end of his contract. He would, however, return in 1610 with Poutrincourt, at which point he continued his work as if he had never ceased it, planting wheat and vines and developing other agricultural projects. Louis's second stint in the New World lasted until 1613, when Englishmen from Virginia, led by Samuel Argall, came north with the goal of sabotaging French interests. First, they sacked the Port-Royal habitation, forcing Louis and the other Frenchmen to flee homeward; they then returned a month later to burn the colony to the ground.

Back in Paris, Louis returned to his normal life and tried to enjoy it. He sold cures and potions to the city locals and looked after his wife and children. Meanwhile, in the New World, French claims were hanging on by a hair. The settlement of Quebec, which Champlain had founded in 1608, didn't have the makings of a true colony. There were no women and no children, and thus none of the institutions that served to promote and support existence beyond the span of a single generation. Those residing there were fur trappers, missionaries, and a ragtag group of soldiers — about fifty men in all. It was the only jewel in France's New World crown, but it was a glorified trading outpost, serving primarily as the waypoint for trade in beaver pelts, which were sent on to the motherland. Champlain, whom Louis had met at Port-Royal, was not going to let the foothold go. Like everyone who knew of Louis's industrious existence at

Port-Royal, Champlain admired the man, and likely informed him of his plan to raise funds for the further development of Quebec.

In 1617, the company of New France traders and merchants (mostly from Rouen and Saint-Malo) that Champlain had founded made Louis a concrete offer to return to the colony: two hundred livres per year for three years, as well as ten acres of land to build a home and to use as he pleased. It was a coup — Louis signed immediately, sold his house on the Seine, and prepared his wife, Marie, and his three children (Guillaume, Guillaumette, and Anne) to depart for wilder pastures. But when the Héberts arrived at the port of Honfleur ready to board the ship, Louis quickly discovered that he had been hoodwinked. The company refused to let the family board unless he signed a modified contract, which reduced his salary to three hundred livres over only two years and required him to farm his ten acres and sell his agricultural output to the company at French market rates. He would also have to serve as the colony's pharmacist, doctor, and surgeon for free at the end of his two-year pay period, earning his living from the farm alone. We cannot know how long Louis hesitated, aghast and furious, before capitulating. What we know is that he indeed signed the new contract and boarded the ship, from whose wooden deck he would have seen the misty coastline of his motherland for the last time.

The Héberts arrived in Quebec in the sweltering splendour of July, when the colony's cliffs would have glimmered a radiant green against the rough navy of the St. Lawrence. Louis, the first private individual to receive a land grant in New France, chose a ten-acre plot comprising what is now the grounds of the Seminary of Quebec and of the Basilica of Notre-Dame. He built his house from wood, and three years later, with the help of the company, he built another from stone. Together with his son, Guillaume, and an indentured servant whose name has been lost to history, he cleared the land and sowed it with wheat, corn, and various herbs. He planted apple and plum orchards and cultivated a vineyard. And his labours were difficult, not least because the company had fought against him clearing the forest on his property, given how essential forested areas were to fur trapping. He was, according to Champlain himself, the first European to live off the land in the New World.

Louis persevered. Being the first apothecary and true colonist in Canada, and thus the only man in the colony to be living off what he could grow and be accompanied by his family, he quickly racked up a number of other firsts. He was the first to import a plough ox from France. His daughter Anne became the first European to be married in New France, and thus Louis became the first European to be made a father-in-law there. The list, as we learn it in elementary and high schools across Quebec, goes on. Typically, it tends to downplay the work that the qualifiers "European" and "colonial" do in its calculation of firsts. Louis himself might have been reluctant to accept such recognition: it is said that he, more than his fellow colonists, was on good terms with the First Nations members around him, believing as he did that they knew best how to cultivate their native soil, and that their traditional medicines would be easier to grow there. (Back in 1611, he was alleged to have cured Actodin, son of the Mi'kmaq chief, from a fatal illness, and to have subsequently provided palliative care to the chief himself, Membertou. Some evidence of his good relations with First Nations members comes, in the biographies, from the fact that, after Louis's death, Marie served as godmother to Naneogauchit, son of the chief of the Innu, then called Montagnais, on the occasion of the latter's baptism; the ceremony was followed by a feast hosted on Hébert lands, featuring a massive cauldron in which were boiled fifty-six bustards, thirty ducks, twenty teals, a quantity of game, two barrels of peas, a barrel of pancakes, twenty pounds of prunes, six baskets of corn, and some other foodstuffs, followed by a traditional dance.) Then again, whatever his reluctance to claim priority and superiority when it came to those lands completely foreign to him and the company, Louis seemed to have no qualms being named the first "sieur" in Quebec, by royal decree. Like any old noble lord presiding over his ten acres (plus some new territory on the Saint-Charles River), he likely enjoyed collecting rents, profiting from the output of his workers, and smiling from his private pew at church.

I hope he enjoyed it while it lasted. That was about four years, at the end of which he died his very Canadian death. During that time, it is almost certain that he made some important contributions to French botanical knowledge of Canadian plants and their uses. He was responsible, for example, for bringing the American groundnut, the meadow-rue, and Canadian wild ginger — all of which have documented medicinal uses — to French attention. Louis might have done much more, if he hadn't, one fine winter's day in 1627, slipped on a patch of ice, hit his head, and died.

◈ ◈ ◈

To a certain subset of Montrealers, Louis Hébert is a sort of Adam, and Marie his Eve. Their descendants likely number in the tens of thousands across Quebec, Ontario, Manitoba, and several American states. As a kid I couldn't help but envy those French Canadians who claimed this or similar heritages — descendants of *les filles du roi*, as they were collectively known, even if this was historically untrue in some cases.* I envied them because, though all of us were born and raised in Quebec, only *they* were Québécois.

* The term, meaning literally "the king's daughters," refers to the approximately eight hundred young French women sent to New France at the behest of Louis XIV, between 1663 and 1673. The scheme originated with Jean Talon, the intendant of New France, who convinced the king that the growth of the colony could be assured by sending marriageable women there to start families with the existing settlers and to encourage more Frenchmen to emigrate to the New World. The women, most of whom were between the ages of twelve and twenty-five, came predominantly from Paris, Normandy, Brittany, and other western regions of France.

I learned this fact quickly and without anyone having to tell me. In the year of my birth, after a referendum on Quebec becoming a sovereign nation narrowly failed, the leader of the Parti Québécois, Jacques Parizeau, blamed the loss on "money and ethnic votes." (Later, in an attempt to explain himself, he seemed to think he was improving his case by claiming that "it is not healthy in a society such as ours that groups, particularly when they come from specific cultural communities, vote 95 percent in the same direction.") At ski school, as a twelve-year-old, I was asked by a boy named Guillaume whether my parents would one day move our family to "*ton pays juif.*" During my brief attempt to play hockey, our scrimmages at practice were usually five-on-five set pieces of *les québécois* versus *les autres.* (I grew up in a relatively bilingual suburb, so the sides were fairly matched.) Fifteen years later, during the pandemic, my downstairs neighbour would invite me to his garden for a few drinks. We lived stacked in a duplex on rue Rivard, in the Plateau, where progressive politics were supposed to reign. My neighbour had also invited over his friend, who proceeded (more belligerently as the night wore on and the case of beer emptied) to question me about where I was really from. I had three grandparents who had been born in North America, I told him, and two of them had even been born right here in Montreal. He proceeded to point to my nose, which to him indicated ulterior origins and filiations. "What about Israel?" he asked. What about it? I pointed out that I was more of a Montrealer than he was: his entire family, so he had explained, lived in Rimouski and had done so for generations. He himself had only come to the city for his bachelor's degree.

It was in fact useless to argue. We both understood his point: this wasn't a matter of citizenship or even lived experiences, but of ethnicity. Despite simply descending from the weaker settler colonial power in an eighteenth-century contest with England, many Québécois see themselves as comprising a sort of indigenous nation. This was made plain in the English-language debate during the 2021 federal election: Yves-François Blanchet, leader of the Bloc Québécois, responded to a question about how Canadians could trust the federal government after 150 years of lies, violence, and abuse toward Indigenous Peoples (preceded by centuries of the same under the empire) by asserting that "no one should tell any nation what to do and that every nation, including Quebec, should be recognized as such and treated like an equal." Many balked at the comparison; but not as many as one might have hoped. The Québécois are unique among North American identity groups in feigning ignorance, when convenient, as to how they really got there. For the rest of us, if one is not wholly or partly Indigenous, one was at some point an immigrant (at best) or a colonizer (at worst).

The focus, for many French-Canadians, is instead on the discrimination that they faced for a couple of hundred years under English rule, after New France was given over to George III in 1763 under the Treaty of Paris. Those francophones who remained at that time in Lower Canada, as it came to be called, were mostly peasants, homesteaders, and poor civil servants — the French nobility having fled back to the Old World. The now-debunked theory that the motto of Quebec, *Je me souviens* — found on government buildings and on every license plate in the province — is the first line of a folk song that goes, "*Je me souviens / Que né sous le lys / Je croîs sous la rose*" (I remember / that born under the lily / I grew up under the rose), was popular for so long because of its utter plausibility. What more romantic vision of one's own victimhood than a caged-bird lyric trying to see the blue sky on the other side of the English boot? But this is exactly what *Je me souviens*, the version unattached to any such song, is meant to convey anyway. In what context is it an act of quiet defiance to remember, if not a past wrongdoing, an erstwhile victimhood?

This peculiar form of self-mythologization has allowed Québécois nationalists to wave a kind of behavioural hall pass that will be familiar to once-victimized groups that suddenly find themselves wielding the machinery of state. The required contortion is simple: the historical fact of having once been victimized is dehistoricized, allowing for identification with the label "victim" in a perennial manner; this way, even from positions of absolute authority, the victim and his victimhood are inalienable. This relationship is also construed as primary, meaning that anyone suffering from the tyranny of the "victim" only has a second-order claim to victim status. The first act of victimization needs to be reconciled before the second can even be considered; until then, no wrong can be done. This accounts for statements like Blanchet's even being thinkable. (Who, exactly, does he think routinely told First Nations people "what to do" during the 150-odd years of French settler colonialism?) And it probably accounts for the fact that, according to a 2015 Angus Reid poll, Quebec Christians were "exceptional," on the question of how each major faith views the others, "for the relatively lower ratings assigned to Muslims, Sikhs and Jews."

The irony and ungainliness of the nationalist reverse victimization narrative is most aptly illustrated by a pair of events that once animated the French-Canadian literary world. On March 27, 1970, at the théâtre Gesù in Montreal, a few thousand revelers gathered to hear about fifty French-Canadian writers recite their poetry. *La nuit de la poésie*, as it was called, was the direct expression of the shifting cultural winds of the 1960s in Quebec and in North America more broadly. It took place three years after Charles de Gaulle caused a minor diplomatic calamity by declaring, from the balcony of Montreal's city hall, "*Vive le Quebec libre!*" More broadly, it represented the energies driving the Quiet Revolution, a period spanning the 1960s to the mid-1970s during which, step by step, the younger generations of Québécois were at the vanguard of wrenching their province away from longstanding Catholic conservatism. The fervour for feminism and Québécois sovereignty was at its crest in 1970, and the night of recitals was itself an opportunity to speak against not only the patriarchy, but the hegemony of English Canada and the English language. On this occasion, Michèle Lalonde recited her poem "Speak White," which audaciously compares the plight of French Canadians to that of Jewish and Black North Americans. It is a provocative piece that asserts the radicalism of that burgeoning movement. (And it was of a feather with Pierre Vallière's *White Niggers of America*, a screed of the same ideas published two years earlier.) The atmosphere, captured by a documentary crew with its finger on the cultural pulse, was electric.

Compare this with the second *nuit de la poésie*, held exactly ten years later. Like all sequels, it sought to recapture something, to go beyond nostalgia and, in effect, reproduce the magic of the original. The 1980 event, by contrast with the first, was a ghost before it began, lesser because it was a copy, an attempt to recapture that original gestalt. The same documentary crew was asked to film the reading; many of the same poets were invited; the same atmosphere was sought. The poets' desire was nostalgic but also, one senses, anxious — anxious to be, still, the kind of poets they had been ten years earlier: those for whom the fight is not yet over.

But it *was* over. In 1977, the Assemblée Nationale du Quebec — under the first nationalist government in the province — passed The Charter of the French language, otherwise known as Bill 101, which made French the official language of Quebec. Within a handful of years, the very future of the province and of its crown jewel, Montreal, was dissolved and replaced. Where one once saw a sprawling city of international import, a hub of the global capitalist, multilingual modernity that Expo 67 had envisioned, one now discovered a daily drain of migrants and businesses heading for the more level waters of Ontario or New York. The anglophones, in a sense, had gone. The French had won.

This made for an awkward night of radical French poetry under a newly francophone state. There was still a viable nationalist position that sought absolute sovereignty: the separation of Quebec from Canada and the establishment of a nation-state. But this was already the doomed mandate of the provincial government in power. It was a dominant idea among the authorities. How, then, to proclaim it without losing one's credibility as a counterculture? A few of the poets present, like Raôul Duguay, returned to the same upholstery that, ten years prior, had suitably garbed his radical hippie ideals. But the return smacked of the farcical: retaking the stage with long hair and a bright rainbow stitched onto his white smock, Duguay cut the same figure but lacked the same force; the animalistic, Yoko Ono–esque chantings that provided the explosive opening to *la nuit* in 1970 had, in 1980, become the perfunctory, environmental vocalizations of a foley artist.

The best of the poets there, including Marie Uguay, intelligently came prepared to direct their political energies elsewhere than toward Québécois nationalism. In a meditation on Cézanne's still life paintings of apples and oranges, Uguay opens her heart to the global wretched of the earth:

> And yet there exist apples and oranges
> Cézanne holding in one hand
> all the fecund amplitude of the earth
> the beautiful vigor of fruit
> I do not know all the fruits by heart
> nor the beneficent warmth of fruit on a white sheet

But hospitals are endless
factories are endless
lines in the frost are endless
beaches turned to marshes are endless

I have known those who suffered until breathlessness
who die endlessly
listening to the voice of a violin or that of a crow
or those of maples in April

Uguay herself was sensitive to the feelings of marginalization internalized among French-Canadians. But she understood equally well that her politics could achieve salience only on the international, rather than the national, plan. Thus, all that she bemoans as "endless," including the "Women endlessly sewing up men / and men pouring a drink," are globalized phenomena. If, in 1970, the language of international struggle was the pathway into Québécois nationalism, at *la nuit* in 1980, for those who could see the need to reposition, the inverse was true: the sentiments of nationalism must give way, rhetorically, to the language of international struggle so as not to be dead on arrival, so as not to protest too much. Fittingly, then, for Uguay the famous two solitudes of language become, in her world-oriented gaze, the two solitudes of man and woman: "Now, I see *the sexes* as two intolerable solitudes."

Some radical nationalists returned and remain. And since 1980, they have been radicals in name only. But that name has counted for a lot. The notion that French and the Québécois identity are "endangered" has long allowed the provincial government to wave away unsettling statistics on discrimination, like the fact that, according to Heritage Canada, "Employers are about 60% more likely to interview a job applicant with a francophone-sounding name in Quebec, despite similar education, experience and skills." This is all in an effort to preserve an embattled identity. The sons and daughters of Hébert have re-conquered their territory, after many long years, and are prepared to defend it to the hilt, more or less. And what else are they to do? *Should they give it all up? Should they compromise on history's gift?* It's a good one; perhaps you've heard it before.

II

One month ago, my parents concluded their sale of the home in which I was raised. They had owned it for thirty years. In that time, they replaced the garage door once (I had dented it hundreds of times with street hockey balls), expanded the basement (where I would host three house parties over the course of my time at high school), renovated each of the bedrooms, and converted an indoor hot tub area, which had been installed by the previous owner, into a home office (sensible). The house sits on a street named for the great Scottish essayist, Thomas Carlyle. It is intersected at one end by a street named for the Battle of Waterloo and at the other end by a circular park, where I spent a good deal of my childhood, named for English businessman Robert Molesworth Kindersley, First Baron Kindersley. In fact, most of the street names in that suburb, known as the Town of Mount-Royal, are named for nineteenth-century English and Scottish notables. The town itself, glimpsed by a passing bird or an airplane, is laid out like a Union Jack, with (Alexander) Laird and (George Perry) Graham boulevards forming the Cross of Saint Andrew (or else the Cross of Saint Patrick, depending on whom you ask).

The Town of Mount-Royal, or TMR as it is known, was a very anglo idea. And despite now being home to more francophones (43 percent) than anglophones (28 percent), it remains an anglo idea. It was established in 1912 by the Canadian Northern Railway to fund the blasting of a tunnel through Mount Royal. TMR would, via this tunnel and its railway, become connected to downtown Montreal, thereby establishing its desirability as a suburb in which to live, a model community reflecting the principles of a so-called garden city, after the era's fashion.

The simultaneously literal and symbolic structuring of Quebec lands according to British designs in service to certain ideals and, above all, to economic growth was merely the continuation of a 150-year-long custom. In 1763, after the Treaty of Paris ended the Seven Years' War and officially gave the British Empire possession of Canada, the latter began dismantling and restructuring the way of life previously enjoyed by the sixty thousand *Canadiens* now inhabiting what the British had begun to call Quebec. Most famously, they took aim at the seigneurial system, which formed a semi-feudal economy that, in exchange for reducing inequalities between lords and their peasants, had kept the economy of the region depressed relative to the British colonies in what are now the United States.* The seigneuries were replaced by townships, which represented a novel and uncomfortable form of life for their newfound residents. Nor was the legal system spared: *Canadiens* used to French civil law now found themselves subject to English common law, which governed everyone on the eastern seaboard from Quebec to Georgia. Finally, the most significant symbolic blow to French life came in

* The seigneuries were primarily defined by a single mutual obligation between the *seigneur* and his *habitants*: the former would build and maintain a gristmill on his lands for use by his tenants; the latter would use *only* this gristmill to grind their grain. Other obligations included a duty of a fixed amount of ground grain owed to the landlord, as well as a fixed number of days of forced labour on the seigneur's lands. Beyond these ties, lord and peasant alike were effectively unbound to one another. *Habitants* could use their lands however they liked, for the most part. They could even stop working altogether, so long as they met their dues. The system was "free" enough that the seigneurs, even at their most demanding, never quite managed to attain a high enough income from their lands to enable them to live independently from them. They moreover retained the habit of importing comfort and luxury goods from France, rather than spending their money domestically, a familiar pattern of consumption that has, as a rule, always stunted the economies where it has been found.

the form of the Oath of Supremacy, which *canadien* political and ecclesiastical office seekers had to take in order to assume their offices, and which proclaimed the English monarch's supremacy over all matters spiritual and religious. Concretely, for the French Canadians this meant renouncing their fealty to the pope and consequently their Catholic faith — in word if not in deed.

Growing up in Quebec, I was used to the idea that these changes fundamentally represented a form of oppression; that, indeed, they represented the oppressive nature of the British Empire in Canada, which found other ways of life to be intolerable and sought to eliminate them by force or assimilation. This was, of course, how the British operated by way of various stratagems worldwide; and even where they got their colonies in line, they never ceased to remind the locals that their fundamentally foreign way of life was less valuable — it is because of such beliefs that the British Empire allowed and induced tens of millions of Indians to starve to death between 1880 and 1920.

But this perspective can only be held so categorically in the case of Canada by eliding a significant part of the context in which the changes to *canadien* society were produced. The 1763 Royal Proclamation, which instituted those very upheavals to the economy, the law, and the social fabric, also ceded huge swaths of the territory east of the Mississippi, formerly belonging to France, to Native Americans. There was no benevolence to this: after years of fighting with and against various Indigenous Peoples, and especially after suffering meaningful defeats in battle during the multifarious uprising, in the summer of 1763, now known as Pontiac's War, the British concluded that total separation from the "Indians" was a bright idea.* The resulting Proclamation Line devoted all of present-day

* They had begun drafting the Royal Proclamation before the outbreak of war with the coalition of Odawa, Potawatomi, Ojibwe, Mingo, and other peoples. The fighting only proved the necessity of separation.

Wisconsin, Michigan, Indiana, Illinois, Ohio, Kentucky, Tennessee, Mississippi, Alabama, and Florida, as well as parts of what are now Minnesota, Vermont, New York, Pennsylvania, West Virginia, Virginia, North Carolina, and Georgia, to the Native Americans.

The Royal Proclamation, conceived to deal with an unruly coalition of neighbours and an ungainly new territorial acquisition, was about self-serving stability more than cultural supremacy. To understand this is to understand that the British were more bent on conflict management and economic order (the one naturally facilitating the other) than on snuffing out French customs and ways of life. This is a fact further proven by the 1774 Quebec Act, devised to quell discontent among the *Canadiens*, who were ripe for being recruited to the side of the Thirteen Colonies then on the precipice of revolt. The act, which sought to mollify the French Canadians by reestablishing their civil law, rewriting their version of the Oath of Supremacy to allow for their Catholic faith, and reneging on plans to abolish the seigneurial system, also aimed to keep the French Canadians from further stoking the fires of rebellion further south — but it had the unintended effect of making the American colonists *more* insubordinate. It became known among Americans as one of the Intolerable Acts — which were passed as a means of punishing the Massachusetts colonists after the Boston Tea Party by repealing many of the rights that guaranteed their self-governance and promoted their economic independence — in part because it was passed during the same parliamentary session as them, but also in part because it granted Quebec some of the lands formerly promised to Native Americans (which might otherwise have gone to landowners in the Thirteen Colonies) and established a stronghold for Catholicism on the continent. It was probably most intolerable to the First Nations whose hard-won territorial gains charted by the Proclamation Line were contravened in order to appease the *Canadiens.*

◈ ◈ ◈

We could continue a tally with the aim of determining just *how* oppressed the French Canadians really are and were. And there is no doubt that, to a considerable degree from 1763 until the francophone nationalists regained political power over Quebec, they were. But in truth the question of oppression is the wrong question. The whole thing is rather a matter of winners and losers in a global game no one wants to play any longer. One colonial power was succeeded by another. It is true that the British did not make life as easy for the francophones under their dominion as it would have been had the French retained control of their conquests; it is true that, at many times, the British made life quite difficult for them.

The history of conflict between the French and the English in Canada from the end of the eighteenth century proceeds in pendulum-like movements that will be familiar to any Canadian schoolkid, with the British seeking to consolidate economic power and political control, and the French seeking to leverage their demographic advantage from below. Generally speaking, throughout the nineteenth century, British policy regarding Canada sought, in part, to offset the demographic imbalance that would give French-speaking Canadians a majority say in the future of the country. They wanted to suppress French voices in the fledgling democracy. The francophones retaliated, whenever possible, via the existing democratic apparatuses of state — but these were in frequent flux. Between the Royal Proclamation of 1763, the Quebec Act of 1774, the Constitutional Act of 1791, the Act of Union of 1840, and Confederation in 1867, the amount and weight of representation afforded to the inhabitants of Canada shifted drastically (as did, to be sure, the size of the population). When francophones were in the majority, the British sought to create, via the Act of Union, disproportionate representation (favouring themselves) in the unified Province of Canada. When immigration from the British Isles gave anglophones the demographic advantage, they sought to return to proportional democracy. Naturally, facing obstacles in the realm of discursive politics, French Canadians also retaliated by force, as during the Lower Canada Rebellion, which was bloody and left sections of major Canadian cities in ashes. The first sparks of French Canadian nationalism were in fact made to fly by routine political clashes with English-speaking Canadians — the Constitutional Act, which for the first time created a separated territorial area for francophones, is typically given as the ur-moment for separatists. From these confrontations, French speakers began to fashion themselves into the victims of a centuries-long struggle for democratic liberty and self-determination.

The tide has since turned, of course. In 1976, the separatist Parti Québécois, fuelled by Charles de Gaulle's call for a free Quebec less than a decade earlier, won a majority in the Quebec provincial government for the first time. This was a watershed moment, marking the mainstreaming of Quebec nationalism and the long-dreamed-for victory of the "revenge of the cradle" ideology, a phrase coined to emphasize the high birthrate among French Canadians in the previous century, and thus the notion that via the cradle, rather than immigration — that is to say, via domestic demographic pressure — francophones could take political power over the province for themselves. The PQ's success led thousands of anglophones to leave the city, especially after the passage of the Charter of the French Language, which defined French as the only official language of Quebec, and which francophones saw as a means to make policy reflect the province's 85 percent French majority (at the time) — whereas anglophones saw the bill as a means of icing them out. Indeed, though the PQ fancied themselves social democrats (even applying for membership to the Socialist International), their nationalism became an obstacle to their principles: how could a Canadian province restrict the right of anglophone Canadians, who speak one of the two federally recognized languages, from living, working, and studying in the territory under its domain? This impasse rather naturally and immediately set the question of national sovereignty at the centre of the agenda. But after two failed referenda on the question of separation — the most recent of which, in 1995, lost by 1 percent of the vote — the separatist factions of the Quebec government, along with their sympathizers and fellow travellers, are no closer to escaping the paradox of attempting to be a nation-state within a nation-state.

The current government of Quebec, knowing that the dream of national sovereignty has to lie dormant for a time (due to its relative unpopularity even among francophones), has set its sights on the remaining linguistic privileges afforded to anglophones in the province. Although Canada is officially a bilingual country, inhabitants of Quebec are only allowed to receive an anglophone education and provincial government services in English if they belong to the community of "historic anglos," the precise meaning of which has remained vague, but the gist of which is that those whose parents went to school in English need not worry. What sounds like a protection of "historic" status is actually a means of ensuring that anyone who is a newcomer to the province — or the child of a newcomer — will not have the option to interact with their government in English, or study in English, no matter their maternal language. Add to this the progressive defunding of English-language colleges and a host of other policies designed to make English scarce in a province beset on all sides by anglophones. The government is providing for — even inadvertently encouraging — a new generation of victims to fashion itself.

◈ ◈ ◈

These, then, are our so-called two solitudes. Forever at odds, forever exchanging the upper hand. It is a term we owe to the last century, when the question of what it meant to be Canadian, rather than a British subject, was thrown into relief by the two world wars. In 1914, Canada was automatically entered into the global conflict when the United Kingdom declared war on Germany, because the country was technically a dominion of the British Empire. This produced, not three years later, a conscription crisis characterized by a sizable portion of the French-speaking population of Canada not wanting to fight for an empire with which they had no affinity — and toward which many of them had only feelings of animosity. British and Canadian leaders learned from this crisis in the interwar period. The Westminster Statute of 1931, passed into law by the British legislature, gave Canada autonomy over its own foreign policy. Though most anglophone Canadians wanted to join Britain's second declaration of war against Germany, on September 1, 1939, Prime Minister William Mackenzie King made it a point to exercise the fresh autonomy granted by the Westminster Statute to determine the timing and manner of Canada's involvement. King waited ten days to enter the Second World War.

The novelist Hugh MacLennan was watching these developments closely. He likely paid particularly close attention to the second conscription crisis, which occurred in 1944 along similar lines to the first, and which proved to King and others in his camp that French Canadian apathy was not merely directed at Britain, but toward anglophone Canada writ large. To fight for the glory of Canada became a difficult proposition for the likes of MacLennan. For there were not one but two Canadas; they inhabited the same sovereign territory but held diverging views of global and domestic politics, and nurtured different and often mutually exclusive lines of affinity with the other nations of the world. They were two solitudes, thesis and antithesis, seeking synthesis in the concept "Canada."

MacLennan's 1945 novel *Two Solitudes* opens unforgettably in the midst of a great flow: "Nowhere has nature wasted herself as she has here. There is enough water in the Saint Lawrence alone to irrigate half of Europe, but the river pours right out of the continent into the sea."

The great Canadian river is symbolic of the many wild and wasteful currents to which human beings are subjected: the passage of time, the transport of ideological conviction, the rapture of love. In a way possibly lost on MacLennan, it is also a metaphor for the very idea of the two solitudes — that of English and French Canada — and its discursive extravagance. How many words have we wasted on asserting the supposedly foundational nature of this divide? How much of that energy has fed nothing, nourished no one, diverted uselessly, dissipated asea? Like the St. Lawrence itself, a river of vitriol flows hard athwart the island of Montreal and past the cliff towns dotting the gulf.

How long until we understand that these are not the only two solitudes that structure our history? Canada is not unique. Like every other Western country in the nineteenth and twentieth centuries, it invited and suffered the growing pains produced by industry. It nurtured capitalists and raised labour like grain. This, more than any other, is the social reality most central to MacLennan's novel. The language question is merely a proxy for a deeper economic question. Within the fictional, rural parish town of Saint-Marc-des-Érables, in Quebec, the changes that will set the course for Québécois politics for the modern era are seeded: Athanase Tallard, the father of the novel's protagonist, attempts to industrialize the sleepy, Church-dominated Saint-Marc and pays the ultimate social price for it. Tallard has, in effect, internalized the Protestant ethic of business, represented in the novel by the city of Montreal, and sought to infuse it into a French, Catholic culture still dominated by a pre-industrial mode of existence. And he is ostracized for it.

Tallard's son, Paul, is the novel's true protagonist because he represents the ambivalence of its central dilemma: how to live between two solitudes. Or else: how to force an overlap, however slight, between them. What might be read as a Bildungsroman that takes its hero through two prejudicial landscapes, each dominated by a language and a religion, is in fact a thinly veiled portrait of a socioeconomic order in flux. Paul, who falls in love with an English-speaking Protestant named Heather, loses his job during the Great Depression, like many French Canadians. He is a suspect figure to Heather's parents not simply because of his father's language and religion, but because these characteristics are taken to mean that he will remain jobless and leech off Heather's inheritance. He is not only *presumed* to be a no-good member of the proletariat; he and his kin from Saint-Marc are literally proletarianized by the encroachment of English business- and landowners upon the town. Rather than being an assertion of a Canadian identification (over and above either a franco-Catholic or anglo-Protestant identification), Paul's decision at the end of the novel to enlist in the Canadian military and fight the Nazis is in fact the fulfillment of the ultimate capitalist ruse: the proletarian offers his life to the state in exchange for an ideological fantasy, otherwise known as honour, that makes his condition bearable. If he returns alive, his sacrifice will only make him more committed to the social order that daily exploits him and divides him against his countrymen, and his service will only make him more productive to that order. He plans, in fact, to become a writer and commit a literary representation of his society to the ranks of mythology — much like MacLennan himself.

Anyone who has been to Montreal can see plainly that, like anywhere else, the two solitudes are in fact the rich and the poor. The city is overlooked by the homes of Outremont (61 percent French-speaking) and Westmount (69 percent English-speaking). To be convinced that what divides us is language is to fail to grasp the difference between the contingent and the essential. If the class divide once fell along linguistic lines, it no longer does so. In fact, if anything the current data show that the income and employment disparity now goes the other way around. A Paul Tallard born today might be heir to a French-owned business; it might be his Heather whose motives are scrutinized.

III

And so we have two competing visions of the two solitudes: one cultural, the other economic. The Third Solitude is the gap between these visions. It is a liminal zone whose inhabitants are not admitted into either vision except as invisible entities.

Between Paul and Heather, there was once a Jew. His father, perhaps, had come from Bessarabia by boat in the 1920s; his mother from Mykolaiv a decade earlier, as a child. Perhaps they or their own parents had been spooked by several decades of pogroms. They spoke Yiddish and Russian at home and were reluctantly picking up English and French with heavy accents. They settled on rue Esplanade in Montreal, in a part of the city filled with other people like them, from places very similar to their homelands. They connected with a local synagogue, which helped to inform them of work and educational opportunities and even trained them in some of the local trades — tailoring, cobbling, grocering, and so on. The

Jew's father, who was literate but not highly educated, tried his luck at fruit selling, buying from a wholesaler at Central Station and selling from a stand in the Plateau. His mother ran the home economy and kept his father's books. She haggled with the wholesaler, ensured that deliveries ran on time, and dealt with creditors; she put aside money, went to market, cooked, cleaned, and changed diapers. They had two children, the boy and his sister. The boy they forced to learn the violin. They forbade him from playing hockey with his friends in the ruelles of the neighbourhood, insisting that he focus on the fiddle; his friends called him "Beethoven Joe." (One afternoon, he snuck out to join them and broke his thumb; he hid his injury from his parents, and would forever have a crooked digit, which he would hold up while telling the story of how it got that way to his grandchildren.) The boy's family was poor but getting a little less poor day by day. Eventually, his mother took the money she had saved and bought a cramped, cold-water flat with it. Later, she bought a few more. She became a landlord, renting to Jews just like herself, who immigrated a little later than herself and needed a place to land and raise their families. The flats were basic, primitive; the tenants had to wash themselves at the local bathhouse on Saint-Laurent. Many of them worked where they lived, at the shops and storefronts in the Plateau and Mile End.

The boy was smart and did well at school; eventually he became one of four Jewish students admitted to his year at McGill Medical School (the university's Jewish quota would remain in place until the late 1960s, when the boy would already be a man with three children). He earned his degree and specialized in neurology, beginning his career-long practice at the Jewish General Hospital, which had been established (back when the boy was just a toddler) as a place of work for Jewish doctors, because the city's Catholic doctors did not want to work with them — a fact made plain to all throughout the so-called Days of Shame in 1934, during which thirty-two resident doctors at the Hôpital Notre-Dame walked off the job and refused to treat patients in protest of the hospital having hired a Jewish intern, Dr. Samuel Rabinovitch. After Dr. Rabinovitch was forced to resign and flee to Missouri for a time, the striking doctors returned to work without sanction or repercussion. The Université de Montréal, where Dr. Rabinovitch had trained, was greatly affected by these protests; in response to them, it instituted restrictions ensuring that Jewish prospective students would have greater difficulty gaining admission to the university. In retrospect, after making it, the boy would come to see himself as a member of a "model minority," having achieved the kind of upward class mobility enjoyed by a startling number of his generation's Jews. With his wife, Eva, he bought a semi-detached house in the Town of Mount-Royal, a bourgeois, middle-class suburb of the city, the Jewish population of which had grown just large enough to merit the building of a small synagogue, Beth-El, designed by the uncle of his future daughter-in-law. Returning now and then to the Plateau — perhaps to eat at Schwartz's Delicatessen, or to have his children's school uniforms tailored, or to re-sole his wife's shoes, or to buy three pounds of fish — he noted with increasing clarity that he was also a lapsed member of a dying breed: the working-class Montreal Jew. Just like when he was a boy, the city's anglo-Protestants and franco-Catholics descended upon the Main for high-quality goods and services at a low price, before returning to their mansions on the hill or their modest homes farther east. But now, with each visit, he could see the neighbourhood change: the cold-water flats became hot-water flats; the Jews became Greeks, who became Portuguese, who became Vietnamese. The boy was no longer a boy, and his community was no longer *that* community. The boy died an old man in 2017, two years after the oldest family-run business on Saint-Laurent, Berson's, a Jewish gravestone manufacturer, closed down, a fact about which the old man was blissfully ignorant, owing to advanced dementia. After ninety-three years, Berson's were unavailable to make the headstone of a boy who had grown up two blocks away.

The life of the boy, Israel Libman, my paternal grandfather, indexes a salient feature of the Third Solitude: it belongs to transients, and is no one's for long. It is like a hallway lined with windows, and out of those windows you can see a North American city like any other, and you can see one dominant culture warring with another for political supremacy, and the two cultures look back at you — at times in bewilderment, at others for support — and for a moment you feel yourself on the outside. You are not a part of it, not really, even if you might want to be. You look to your left and your right and see your comrades, and say, "This is a community, we the aliens are a community." But all the while you are moving along the hallway; it is hard work, but you do it; you are poor, but you do it. At the end of that hallway is a door, beyond which there are no more windows; there is just the world. And *this* world, the one of the two solitudes, sucks you in and breaks you apart. It never forgets who you were, back when it saw you peering from the hallway; and you never forget that once you had comrades at your shoulders. But you're in the world, now, and there are others now in the hallway who look out at you and witness you in pitched battle, and ask: "Why does he speak English and not French and not his own language either?" "Why does she not know a trade?" "Why do they no longer side with people like us, who move through the hallway, as they once did?"

The reality of the Jewish Third Solitude is merely the *memory* of the Jewish Third Solitude. It is not us, today, but another. We came speaking Yiddish, Polish, Russian, German, Spanish, Hungarian, Romanian, Czech, and Lithuanian. We speak English because the Catholics did not want us in their schools. We speak Arabic and Farsi because we came from Iran and Iraq. Or, we speak French because later we came from North Africa (the Catholics still did not want us in their schools). We became a model minority because we worked and studied hard, and because we worked and studied hard, we came into money, and because we came into money, we hoarded it. Like any old class of bourgeois folk, we took it believing it was ours, forgetting that we once worked for hoarders, went on strike with our unions, taught our children socialism, and lived in community. What we choose to remember takes a vestigial form: buildings that used to be synagogues, but are now offices with plaques on them; political movements that used to be progressive, but are now political lobbies that self-mythologize nostalgically about their working-class origins; pedagogical institutions that used to be socialist, used to believe in cultivating a respect for labour and folk traditions and a suspicion of mystifications, but are now conservative schools preaching right-wing Zionism. Some of our grand institutions remain, like the Temple Emanu-El, the reform synagogue to which my family belongs, and the Congregation Shaar Hashomayim, which flourished under the leadership of Lyon Cohen, grandfather to Leonard Cohen. But the ideological pluralism they once represented has narrowed dramatically. If you wanted to hear a great Jewish debate, I couldn't tell you where to go.

Anna Stearns, my great-grandmother, could. But that was back then. Anna was a Zionist, and a staunch one at that. She had followed the war from her strange new home and had lived through a steady trickle (and then a river) of news about dead and missing friends, family, and acquaintances. In her 1981 book, *Essays in Education, Religion and Psychotherapy*, she compares the story of Zionism's fruition to a hero's journey narrative. She resents two currents of Jewish thought from the Old World, with which she would have been intimately familiar: assimilationism and Communism. She blames both of these for obstructing the development of

Zionism: on the one hand, "the Jewish Emancipation from the Ghetto in Germany — although it was mostly a consequence of Napoleonic and French victories — made Jews even greater German patriots than they had ever been," in the period before Hitler's rise; on the other, contemplating the "sins of Russian revolutionaries" and the Jews who partook in them, she wonders "about the amount of self-hatred that some Jewish socialists displayed throughout the years." Anna dwells on these polemics "because many of us would never understand, otherwise, the tremendous obstacles Zionism had to overcome within Jewish communities before it could tackle outside enemies."

And yet, despite such strong and, given the circumstances, understandable feelings about Zionism, she consorted her entire life with the very assimilationists, socialists, and Communists whose ideas she claimed to abhor. She and her husband Eugene spent their postwar years helping displaced European Jews immigrate to Canada; they housed them, clothed them, found them jobs, and played matchmaker in some cases. Eugene hired some of them at his own concrete company, despite their lack of qualifications. He debated with them at the dinner table, bought goods and services from them, exchanged gifts with them, prayed with them on the High Holidays. The Stearns helped these men and women assimilate, and they offered a form of small-c communism to boot. They gave according to their abilities, and their guests received according to their needs. They did this because to be Jewish was an older idea than to be Zionist, was to contain multitudes, and not to harden into ideological amber. They did this because, in the hallways of the Third Solitude, their comrades were at their shoulders, not clambering up the hill for a better view.

◇ ◇ ◇

If you wanted to hear a great Jewish debate, as I said, I couldn't tell you where to go. But I could tell you where to find not one but two gigantic mural portraits of Leonard Cohen. He is perhaps the one figure we can all agree on. Maybe this is because, like our greatest poets, he exiled himself from the city that raised him and that he loved. When he wrote "Montreal," which I've taken as an epigraph to this essay, he was more than a decade into his career and internationally renowned. Yet his mind returned, as ever, to his hometown. When he looked at Montreal, he saw the fish who asks, "What is water?" He saw men, women, and children ignorant of the shared ether they lived in and breathed. He saw factions divided one against the other, unaware that, along some register alive yet unseen by them, they are made whole.

He calls this higher plane The Church. Not the Catholic Church, nor the Protestant one, but a greater structure in which they are but two participants. It is characteristic of Cohen to reach for the vocabulary of religion, and typical of a great poem to create an irresolvable ambiguity between competing meanings (in this case, the word "Church"). He is suggesting that there is some true transcendental structure, older than all faiths, older, even, than the weather — a structure of which "The Church" is a symbol. Cohen is reaching for an archaic natural order, a disembodied higher power built on a foundation of stone more ancient than the mere pebble of a two-thousand-year-old religion, within which all life is invisibly organized. What else could such an order be than a kind of church? The Platonic form, maybe, of every church of every faith humankind has known. For Cohen, the bones of that order, the very elements that uphold it, are visible in a place like Montreal, where internal contradiction between seemingly opposed forces makes way for a synthesis, for some sense of communality that can perhaps only be grasped in the universalizing experience of a harsh winter. The city's strife, in his conception, is an internal necessity. It is a swirling system of antigens and antibodies, striving ultimately to strengthen the lifeblood of the greater whole. The Church of Montreal pits one source of pride against another, and from their mutual destruction only a few glinting parts are salvaged for the myth. The city is neither as Québécois as Quebec City, nor as Canadian as Calgary. It is neither English enough to sustain corporate overdevelopment, nor French enough to stamp out bilingualism. And it has evolved its myth slowly over time, through dozens of waves of immigration and two world wars, through mailbox IEDs, and humanist charters, and language laws. Where once Montrealers dreamed of world's fairs, Olympic Games, and a sprawling economic capital with two airports, now they pine for a baseball team they never watched, build museums to the former glory of their ethnic minorities, and all but ignore the windswept Mirabel airport tarmac from which commercial flights shall never take off. Ours is a solitary, self-contained Church that keeps a distance from external pressures and influences. Yet inside the myth grows; it writes and rewrites itself, steeping us in its values, laws, and perspectives.

Weather over and above history. The winter, as Cohen understood, is the favorite and most reliable executor of The Church's myth, the legend that would subsume the lesser forces of religion, ideology, and politics beneath a transcendent silence. It humbles us and yet makes each of us a fighter. Throughout this wind-whipped season we trudge through slush in search of bus stops and tiptoe carefully over black ice. We reach for our phones less often to keep our hands warm and budget thirty minutes more for our morning commutes. And so the Montrealer's hibernal life is daily reduced to survivalist concerns. All pride is stripped down, all shoulders hunched earward under the weight of winter. There is everywhere a wilderness, one that is ceremoniously established, and yet arable for Brightness. The Brightness of bodies huddled together for warmth under bus shelters, of doors to warm Métro antechambers held open by strangers, of skates scraping the ice under a pre-dinner pickup game, where Beethoven Joe has furtively come to play. The Brightness, put simply, of a community whose pretensions have been cut down by the cold and the wet, and whose path forward cannot accommodate pride, or egotism, or domination. This is how the myth begins and perpetuates itself.

As with any church, here there are rites and there are traditions. We have the rite of festivals, of laughter and of music. In the winter we warm ourselves under our Lady of the Harbour to outdoor nocturnal concerts; in the summer we attend our mass in the Parc du Mont-Royal to the percussions of the Tam Tams. And for tradition, we have corruption. We endure crack-prone construction projects contracted annually to the mafia and our city's corrupt elite. We ask not whether, but to what extent our officials are involved. And it is our lot to complain together, and to laugh together.

And yet the criminality never grows too unbearable, nor do the forces of good win out. Our corporate institutions do not overgrow our cultural ones. Our old lineages are indebted to even older ones, and both must leave room for those newly arrived. For each force is cancelled by another, and The Church inclines toward its inner homeostasis. All have their place in the congregation, where the hymn is no one's and everyone's, and where every man, woman, and child is protected.

If there are two or three solitudes, or if there are as many solitudes as there are people on Earth, then against these Cohen posits a kind of brutal unification beneath The Church. He published "Montreal" in 1978, one year after Bill 101 became law, decreeing that French would be the sole and exclusive language of the province of Quebec. And yet he understood any such law to be subordinate to The Church, a point of pride to be pulled down. It was a force of divisiveness that the higher order could not tolerate, and so would absorb and dissolve into some more universal experience. A Romantic idea, to be sure — but also a mythical one. Cohen would like everything to be subsumed under the myth. The Church, in Montreal, is what sustains us, intoxicates us, and it is why we shall never really leave. We might find ourselves in New York or Paris or, like Cohen, on Hydra. But we are drawn to The Church and we iterate its myth. And if we do not someday return, then we find a way to bring it with us, even if only by letting "Suzanne" seep lazily through our vestibules and bedrooms.

Epilogue

The Rest Is Dross

To have gathered from the air a live tradition
or from a fine old eye the unconquered flame
This is not vanity.
Here error is all in the not done,
all in the diffidence that faltered ...

— **Ezra Pound**

I am not sure whether we are better served by the image of a spiritually transcendent order, or that of a battle between siloed forces: The Church or the solitudes. They are two ways of describing something that is constantly in flux, of inscribing in stone that which is writ in water. So they are doomed to regular failure.

Having come to the end of something, I still find myself grasping in the dark. At the centre of this book, bending the light of my various attempts to regain time past, is a world. I do not mean simply the contained and relatively definable community of Montreal Jews within which I was raised, but rather an ethos that does not belong to any particular geography. It can be found wherever time appears to have ground to a halt, wherever its flow has been dammed, in vain, by ideology.

To Anna and Eugene Stearns, my great-grandparents, this world was the New World; not in the style of the old colonial imagination, but in the style of rebirth and new beginnings that characterizes the refugee imagination. And the moment of their arrival in this new world seems, to me, antediluvian. In 1938, when they arrived in North America, several alternate futures seemed possible. Looking back to that time, as I write this on an overcast summer's day in 2024, I am aware of the ghosts of those futures that never materialized: possible configurations of the world (and the Jews living in it) that had not yet been decided. They were futures that belong to the world of yesterday, brought over by Anna's generation, who always maintained one foot in the new and the other in the old. They were all the various permutations of the what-could-be that had not yet been foreclosed by a dominant ideology. Concretely, they were the visions of Jewish life that had yet to be captured and assimilated into political Zionism: pluralistic belonging in North America, for example; or a global, secular socialism in which traditional cultures and languages were nurtured as syndicates; or even, in a bid to divert the already moving colonial-Zionist project toward a more humane direction, a non-theocratic, multi-national, democratic state in Palestine.

If the process of writing this book has revealed anything, it is that these vanished visions of the future need to be resuscitated. The cost of failing to do so will be the furtherance of untold misery upon Palestinians and Israelis alike, and the continued stultification of North American Jewry, if not Judaism as such. The world of yesterday was home not only to fledgling Zionists. It was home to thousands of Bund members and supporters who knew that Judaism did not depend on a state for its vitality; to Jews living in Ottoman Palestine, who were for the most part non-Zionist and who were content with their cosmopolitan existence, in the words of Rashid Khalidi, "as Jews who were part of the indigenous Muslim-majority society"; and to millions of diasporans who felt that the good fight involved the betterment of life for all, not only themselves, in pluralist and socialist societies that needed to be raised from beneath their feet, not imagined in an elsewhere where others already dwelled.

If after the Second World War, there was a need for a safe haven for the world's remaining Jews, there was never any need for Zionism. At least, not the Zionism that came to pass — that which leveraged the colonial apparatuses of state to take for itself what belonged to others. But the past is past. It is there not to be undone but to be remembered. And insofar as we forget the futures it dreamed of, we forget to dream of futures for ourselves. Anna's New World — our world of today, the one that made me and, consequently, this book — now imagines no future. It sustains itself on an eternal, horizonless present. This is a presentist ideology: the inability to know the past and to see it as having conditioned the current moment; the inability to know the future and to see it as something that can be created; the inability to know the present and see it as something that is always becoming past; and all of this in an infinite movement of recurrence. If the Holocaust is perpetually yesterday and tomorrow, then we neither know nor see the past, present, or future, and we are beset on all sides by horror. Who would dare rejoin the flow of time against such odds?

But I am indulging in fallacies. There is no "rejoining" time, just as there is no damming it. You will be borne ahead whether you will it or not. The greater your insistence on an ideology of the present, the greater your complicity in the ravages that such ideologies wreak to sustain themselves. You are being borne ahead: hour after hour, sentence after sentence. Anna understood this. "The world falls away like wet sand being drawn out into the rip current," she wrote. Yet she refused to stay standing on the shore. The past was not a foreign country to her; she could return there in an instant through memory, with the ethos of a critic; for she knew that it produced the present in which she lived and contained the mistakes she would rectify in her dreams of the future.

We would do well to see in her future our past, and to see in that past the errors we repeat compulsively to bloody ends. The place I came from, the world that was new to Anna but has since lost all novelty, is all seized up; to reanimate it, we must try, as I have vainly done, to recapture that old spirit, sing that old song — to imagine new possibilities for our lives, yes, but also to resurface the old ways of being individuals, Jews, and citizens. Ways that used to obtain in the world of yesterday, and that might yet obtain tomorrow. The next world, our new one, is something we must create daily. We can begin by consigning all that is rotten and wicked to the dustbin.

Acknowledgements

This book would not have made it into the world without the following people, whom I wish to thank. First, I would like to thank the team at Dundurn: Russell Smith, my editor, for giving form where formlessness reigned; my publisher, Meghan Macdonald, for championing this project from its inchoate beginnings as a proposal; Elena Radic, Laura Boyle, and Jennifer Hale for ensuring this ship was seaworthy. I would like to thank my agent, Akin Akinwumi, a visionary, for his steadfast support and guidance. I would like to thank Bruce Robbins, Marguerite Happe, and Celeste Marcus, editors at *Politics/Letters*, the *Rambling*, and *Liberties Magazine*, respectively, for publishing excerpts of *The Third Solitude* (in two of those cases, before I knew I had a book on my hands).

I would like to thank the many people who provided feedback and advice on this book through its various stages of composition, and who have served as indispensable interlocutors for its central themes and ideas over the past few years: Abdelwahab Al Bakri, Ryan Doubiago Bishara, Margaret Cohen, Amir Eshel, Matthew

Friedman, Mark Greif, Brody Hoppenheim, Sarah Kareem, Crystal Lake, Josh Lilien, Alex Marraccini, Stu Mashaal, Mark McGurl, Amber Moyles, Alexander Nemerov, Ryan Ruby, Tobias Ryan, Jacob Shapiro, Michael Sheiner, Hannah Smith-Drelich, Alina Stefanescu, Lisa Wein, and Eric Weinthal.

Thank you to the curators and archivists at the Jüdischer Museum Wien, the Sigmund Freud Museum of Vienna, the Museum of Jewish Montreal, and the Montreal Holocaust Museum, whose collections and exhibitions have informed this book.

Thank you to Veronica and Michael, and to Alex and Cécile, for giving me a home away from home in which to write, in Kalahe and Paris respectively.

This book would have no substance nor *raison d'être* without my family. Thank you to my parents, Michael and Susan, who raised me to be curious and to hold out my hand to the downtrodden; to my brothers Max and Eli, with whom I have been having these conversations (with varying degrees of sophistication on my part) since I was a child; to my relatives in Vienna, who brought Anna's world to life for me; to Rickie and Debbie, whose memories of my great-grandparents have been my archive; to Eric, who, along with my father, has kept the documentary traces of our family preserved and who provided me with many of the photographs and letters mentioned in this book; to Ada, who made the odyssey that preserved our family; and last but foremost, to my two grandmothers, Eva Libman (née Sternschuss) and Joan Kahn (née Yess), who give meaning to it all.

Finally, I would like to thank my partner Camille, my first reader, whose presence can be found on every page, and whose own solitude protects, touches, and greets my own.

Appendix

Family Tree

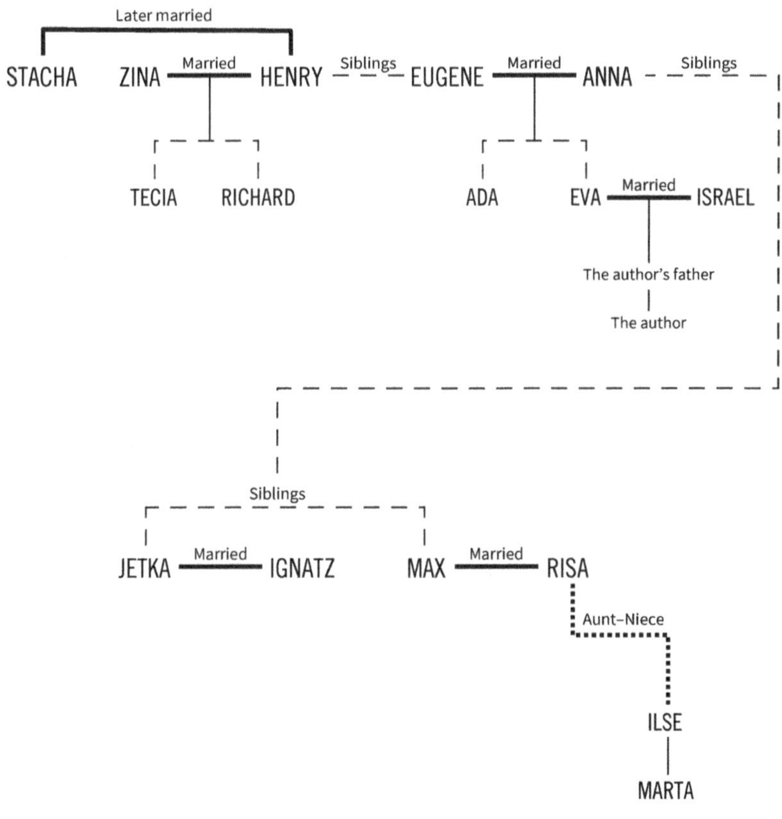

Reading List

Adams, Howard. *Prison of Grass: Canada from a Native Point of View.* Rev. ed. Saskatoon, SK: Fifth House, 1989.

Alroey, Gur. "Journey to New Palestine: The Zionist Expedition to East Africa and the Aftermath of the Uganda Debate." *Jewish Culture and History* 10, no. 1 (2008): 23–58. doi.org/10.1080/1462169X.2008.10512090.

Anctil, Pierre. *History of the Jews in Quebec.* Translated by Judith Weisz Woodsworth. University of Ottawa Press, 2021.

Anderson, Fred. *Crucible of War: The Seven Years' War and the Fate of Empire in British North America, 1754–1766.* New York: Vintage, 2001.

Anonymous. *The First Poems in English.* Edited by Michael Alexander. London: Penguin Classics, 2008.

Arendt, Hannah, and Amos Elon. *Eichmann in Jerusalem: A Report on the Banality of Evil.* New York: Penguin Classics, 2006.

Arendt, Hannah, and Jerome Kohn. *Between Past and Future.* Annotated edition. New York: Penguin Classics, 2006.

Avineri, Shlomo. *Herzl's Vision: Theodor Herzl and the Foundation of the Jewish State.* Translated by Haim Watzman. New York: BlueBridge, 2014.

Bailyn, Bernard. *The Peopling of British North America: An Introduction*. New York: Vintage, 2011.

Barthes, Roland. *Camera Lucida: Reflections on Photography*. Translated by Richard Howard. New York: Hill and Wang, 2010.

Bauman, Zygmunt. *Retrotopia*. Cambridge, MA: Polity, 2017.

Beller, Steven. *Vienna and the Jews, 1867–1938: A Cultural History*. Cambridge: Cambridge University Press, 1991.

Benjamin, Walter. "Berlin Childhood Around 1900." Translated by Howard Eiland. Cambridge, MA: Belknap Press, 2006.

Berger, John. *Ways of Seeing: Based on the BBC Television Series*. London: Penguin Books, 1990.

Bishara, Azmi. *Palestine: Matters of Truth and Justice*. London: Hurst, 2022.

Bishara, Marwan. *The Invisible Arab: The Promise and Peril of the Arab Revolutions*. New York: Bold Type Books, 2012.

Borneman, Walter R. *The French and Indian War: Deciding the Fate of North America*. Illustrated edition. New York: Harper Perennial, 2007.

Bothwell, Robert. *The Penguin History of Canada*. Illustrated edition. Toronto: Penguin Canada, 2007.

Boym, Svetlana. *The Origins of Nostalgia: Memories and Reflections*. London: Bloomsbury Academic, 2023.

—. *The Future of Nostalgia*. New York: Basic Books, 2002.

Camus, Albert. *The Rebel: An Essay on Man in Revolt*. New York: Vintage, 1992.

Celan, Paul. *The Meridian: Final Version-Drafts-Materials*. Edited by Bernhard Böschenstein and Heino Schmull. Translated by Pierre Joris. Stanford: Stanford University Press, 2011.

—. *Selected Poems and Prose of Paul Celan*. Translated by John Felstiner. Illustrated edition. New York, London: W. W. Norton & Company, 2001.

Cohen, Leonard. *Poems and Songs: Cohen*. Edited by Robert Faggen. New York: Everyman's Library, 2011.

Coupland, Douglas. *Generation X: Tales for an Accelerated Culture*. New York: St. Martin's Griffin, 1991.

Davis, Mike. *Late Victorian Holocausts: El Niño Famines and the Making of the Third World*. London: Verso, 2017.

Didi-Huberman, Georges. *Confronting Images: Questioning the Ends of a Certain History of Art*. University Park, PA: Penn State University Press, 2009.

—. *Images in Spite of All: Four Photographs from Auschwitz*. Translated by Shane B. Lillis. Chicago: University of Chicago Press, 2012.

—. *The Surviving Image: Phantoms of Time and Time of Phantoms: Aby Warburg's History of Art*. Translated by Harvey Mendelsohn. University Park, PA: Penn State University Press, 2018.

Eliot, T.S. *Collected Poems: 1909–1962*. London: Faber & Faber, 2002.

Faulkner, William. *As I Lay Dying*. New York: Vintage, 1991.

Frankl, Viktor E. *Man's Search for Meaning*. Boston: Beacon Press, 2006.

Freud, Sigmund. *The Uncanny*. Translated by David McLintock. Illustrated edition. New York: Penguin Classics, 2003.

Hinton, Alexander Laban, Andrew Woolford, and Jeff Benvenuto, eds. *Colonial Genocide in Indigenous North America*. Illustrated edition. Durham: Duke University Press Books, 2014.

Hunt, Lynn. *Inventing Human Rights: A History*. New York: W. W. Norton & Company, 2008.

Kafka, Franz. *The Castle*. Edited by Ritchie Robertson. Translated by Anthea Bell. Oxford: Oxford University Press, 2009.

—. *The Lost Writings*. Edited by Reiner Stach. Translated by Michael Hofmann. New York: New Directions, 2020.

Khalidi, Rashid. *The Hundred Years' War on Palestine*. New York: Metropolitan Books, 2021.

Koselleck, Reinhart. *Futures Past: On the Semantics of Historical Time*. Translated by Keith Tribe. New York: Columbia University Press, 2004.

—. *Sediments of Time: On Possible Histories*. Edited by Sean Franzel and Stefan-Ludwig Hoffmann. Stanford, CA: Stanford University Press, 2018.

Lacoursière, Jacques. *A People's History of Quebec*. Translated by Robin Philpot. Illustrated edition. Montreal: Baraka Books, 2009.

Laqueur, Walter. *A History of Zionism: From the French Revolution to the Establishment of the State of Israel*. New York: Knopf Doubleday Publishing Group, 2003.

Lavsky, Hagit Hadassa. *The Creation of the German-Jewish Diaspora: Interwar German-Jewish Immigration to Palestine, the USA, and England*. Berlin: De Gruyter Oldenbourg, 2018.

Layton, Irving. *A Wild Peculiar Joy: The Selected Poems*. Toronto: McClelland & Stewart, 2004.

L'Encyclopédie Canadienne. "Louis Hébert." Accessed July 15, 2024. thecanadianencyclopedia.ca/fr/article/hebert-louis-1.

MacLennan, Hugh. *Two Solitudes*. 3rd ed. Montreal: McGill-Queen's University Press, 2018.

McCullers, Carson. *Carson McCullers: Stories, Plays & Other Writings*. Edited by Carlos Dews. New York: Library of America, 2017.

Merwin, W.S. *Collected Poems 1952–1993*. Edited by J.D. McClatchy. New York: Library of America, 2013.

Morris, Benny. *1948: A History of the First Arab-Israeli War*. New Haven, CT: Yale University Press, 2008.

Nemerov, Alexander. *Wartime Kiss: Visions of the Moment in the 1940s*. Princeton, NJ: Princeton University Press, 2012.

Nietzsche, Friedrich. *Beyond Good and Evil*. Translated by R.J. Hollingdale. Reissue edition. London: Penguin Classics, 2003.

Pappe, Ilan. *The Ethnic Cleansing of Palestine*. 2nd ed. Oxford: Oneworld Publications, 2007.

Pound, Ezra. *The Cantos of Ezra Pound*. New York: New Directions, 1996.

Rilke, Rainer Maria. *Letters to a Young Poet*. Translated by Charlie Louth. London: Penguin Classics, 2014.

Said, Edward W. *Culture and Imperialism*. New York: Vintage, 1994.

—. *The Question of Palestine*. New York: Vintage, 1992.

Schama, Simon. *The Story of the Jews Volume One: Finding the Words: 1000 BC–1492 AD*. New York: Ecco, 2017.

—. *The Story of the Jews Volume Two: Belonging: 1492–1900*. New York: Ecco, 2020.

Schneer, Jonathan. *The Balfour Declaration: The Origins of the Arab-Israeli Conflict*. New York: Random House, 2010.

Schorske, Carl E. *Fin-De-Siecle Vienna: Politics and Culture*. New York: Vintage, 1980.

Sebald, W.G. *Austerlitz*. 10th anniversary ed. New York: Modern Library, 2011.

Segev, Tom. *1949: The First Israelis*. New York: Simon & Schuster, 2018.

Shakespeare, William. *Shakespeare's Sonnets & Poems*. Edited by Barbara A. Mowat and Paul Werstine. New York: Simon & Schuster, 2006.

Shavit, Ari. *My Promised Land: The Triumph and Tragedy of Israel*. New York: Random House, 2013.

Slucki, David. *The International Jewish Labor Bund After 1945: Toward a Global History*. New Brunswick, NJ: Rutgers University Press, 2012.

Sontag, Susan. *On Photography*. New York: Farrar, Straus and Giroux, 2011.

Stannard, David E. *American Holocaust: The Conquest of the New World*. Rev. ed. New York: Oxford University Press, 1993.

Stein, Gertrude. *Making of Americans*. 3rd ed. Normal, IL: Dalkey Archive Press, 1995.

Stepanova, Maria. *In Memory of Memory*. Translated by Sasha Dugdale. New York: New Directions, 2021.

Uguay, Marie. *Journal*. Translated by Jennifer Moxley. Toronto: Cormorant Books, 2024.

—. *Poèmes*. Montreal: Éditions du Boréal, 2006.

Verlagsanstalt, Evangelische. *The Dresden Frauenkirche: Church Guide*. 3rd ed. Dresden: Evangelische Verlagsanstalt, 2016.

Villon, François. *Œuvres complètes.* Paris: Folio, 2020.

White, Hayden. *Metahistory: The Historical Imagination in Nineteenth-Century Europe.* 40th anniversary ed. Baltimore, MD: Johns Hopkins University Press, 2014.

Wolff, Frank. *Yiddish Revolutionaries in Migration: The Transnational History of the Jewish Labour Bund.* Chicago: Haymarket Books, 2021.

Wordsworth, William. *The Prelude: The Four Texts.* Edited by Jonathan Wordsworth. Rev. ed. London: Penguin Classics, 1996.

Young, James E. *At Memory's Edge: After-Images of the Holocaust in Contemporary Art and Architecture.* New Haven, CT: Yale University Press, 2002.

Zwicky, Jan. *The Experience of Meaning.* Illustrated edition. Montreal: McGill-Queen's University Press, 2019.

About the Author

Photo by Camille Rollason

Benjamin Libman was born and raised in Montreal. His essays, reviews, and fiction have appeared in the *New York Times*, the *Yale Review*, the *London Magazine*, *New Left Review*, the *Guardian*, and elsewhere. He is the co-translator of Gisèle Sapiro's *The Sociology of Literature* (Stanford University Press, 2023). He lives in Montreal and Paris.